Introduction

I hear and I forget.
I see and I remember.
I do and I understand.

—attributed to Confucius[*]

Our choice of the title *Strategize! Experiential Exercises in Strategic Management* highlights the learning basis of the student text. Experiential learning is broadly defined as any activity that students perform and from which they extract learning. It is based on social learning theory, which stresses that individuals develop hypotheses about the relationship between their own behavior and future consequences based on their experience and observations. An important component of this is active learning, which requires students to be "doing things and thinking about the things they are doing." For this reason, active learning—the benefits of which are summed in the quotation above—covers a wide range of activities that include case discussions, simulations, role-playing, and field projects, to name a few.

The teaching of the business policy/strategy course has traditionally relied on various forms of active learning. The predominant method has been the use of business cases. These are lively when there is extensive student participation. However, in our experience, even though students understand the concepts, they are unable to identify how they could be usefully applied in a particular context. In addition, another form of active learning, computer-based simulations, is now used by several instructors, and simulations help the students to effectively develop a general management point of view and to appreciate the trade-off among different functions. These simulations, however, are also somewhat limiting since students rarely get to experiment with appropriate models or concepts before attempting to apply them to simulation specifics.

Recently more textbooks at the end of each chapter provide short exercises for students to perform. These are mostly in the nature of interviewing executives or doing Internet research to gather specific information. While these exercises engage the students in doing things, they do not satisfy an important prerequisite to complete the experiential learning cycle, namely, instructor participation in facilitating the learning.

There are many experiential exercises in different fields based on simple games, and these add an element of fun to the classroom. If they are unstructured, however, they lose their learning value. Experiential exercises need to satisfy certain specific criteria in order to maximize the learning benefits from them. They include:

1. They must have a clear learning objective.
2. They must be designed to elicit specific theoretical and predictable behavior.
3. The instructor plays an active role in conducting the exercise and extracting the learning in a debriefing discussion.
4. The instructor is able to assess the learning through a grading/evaluation mechanism.

---

[*] From J. W. Gentry. 1990. What is experiential learning? In *Guide to Business Gaming and Experiential Learning*, edited by J. W. Gentry, p. 9. East Brunswick, NJ: Nichols/GP.

Following these criteria ensures that certain specific skills and cognition can be developed in the student. This is made possible by specifically structured exercises as developed in our book.

In *Strategize!,* we have put together a set of experiential exercises that serve as a supplement to standard textbooks in the field of business policy and strategy. This manual has been written with the objective of helping the instructor administer the exercise and maximize the learning value for the participants.

Integrating into the Syllabus

Most of the exercises in the student text are designed to fit into a single class session. When the classes are, for example, two hours and 50 minutes long, the first part of the session can be devoted to lecture and case discussion and the second half to an exercise. If the session is 75 minutes, the exercise would fit neatly into it.

To ensure a high level of student participation, we suggest allocating 10 or 15 percent of the grade for exercise work. Most of the grade is based on two components: Whether students come to class having completed the individual aspect of the exercise and the team's work during class.

The matrix in the student text (Figure I.2) will help the instructor identify the specific exercises that supplement chapters of various textbooks. When the exercise is scheduled to follow the session where a particular concept is covered, the student would have the requisite conceptual background. The reading that accompanies each exercise provides a quick review of the concept or model in use.

Team Versus Individual

The notes for each exercise explain how it can be administered on an individual or team basis. In the case of some sessions, the first part of the exercise would be done individually and then discussed within a group. The projects described in Part V of the book are team based. Some instructors prefer to maintain the same team through the whole semester.

Team formation is an important activity that should be given some forethought by the instructor, especially at the beginning of the semester, for it pays off in terms of a better learning experience for the students and less administrative responsibility for the instructor. Principles of cooperative learning, such as maintaining individual accountability and creating a situation in which students rely on one another to achieve a specific outcome, provide techniques to enhance the group experience. In Appendix A of this manual, we describe a process for team formation that could be followed. In Appendix B, we have provided a peer evaluation form that could be administered to the students during or at the end of the semester in order to translate a group grade to individual students.

Debriefing

This is a crucial part of the exercise administration. During most of the exercise, the instructor is providing clarifications on the process, explaining the requirements, and so on. The content and learning are probed during the debriefing. It is important the instructor uses this time to ask questions and guide the discussion on the activity undertaken so that students are able to make the intended connections. Even in situations where a student asks the instructor directly to give

Strategize!

Experiential Exercises in Strategic Management

First Edition

Julie Siciliano

Western New England College

C. Gopinath

Suffolk University

SOUTH-WESTERN

THOMSON LEARNING

Australia · Canada · Mexico · Singapore · Spain · United Kingdom · United States

Instructor's Manual (to accompany *Strategize! Experiential Exercises in Strategic Management, 1e*)
by Julie I. Siciliano & C. Gopinath

VICE PRESIDENT/PUBLISHER:	Jack W. Calhoun
EXECUTIVE EDITOR:	John Szilagyi
MARKETING MANAGER:	Rob Bloom
DEVELOPMENTAL EDITOR:	Judith O'Neill
PRODUCTION EDITOR:	Elizabeth A. Shipp
MEDIA TECHNOLOGY EDITOR:	Vicky True
MEDIA DEVELOPMENTAL EDITOR:	Kristen Meere
MEDIA PRODUCTION EDITOR:	Mark Sears
MANUFACTURING COORDINATOR:	Sandee Milewski
EDITORIAL PRODUCTION AND INTERNAL DESIGN:	James Reidel, LogaTorial Editorial Services
COVER DESIGN:	Rick Moore
COVER IMAGE:	Photo Disc, Inc.
PRINTER:	Globus Printing, Inc.

Printed in the United States of America
1 2 3 4 5 04 03 02 01

For more information contact South-Western, 5101 Madison Road, Cincinnati, Ohio, 45227 or find us on the Internet at http://www.swcollege.com.

For permission to use material from this text or product, contact us by
• telephone: 1-800-730-2214
• fax: 1-800-730-2215
• web: http://www.thomsonrights.com

ISBN: 0-324-07189-2

the correct answer, our preference is to first ask the student to explain the answer he or she has noted on the form. Then, ask if anybody else in class would like to respond. This approach prompts the student to first attempt to make his or her own meaning and enables the instructor to create the environment for shared learning.

In each exercise, we have provided the instructor with details to guide the discussion and with the kind of questions that can be raised to help the participants derive meaning from the exercises.

Prior Preparation Versus In-class Work

For each Strategy Session, it is recommended that the instructor require the students to complete the reading and the case where applicable before coming to class. A few minutes at the start of the exercise can be set aside to refresh the material. Except where specified, we recommend that the completion of forms generally be done in class.

Use of Outside Material

All the information required for the Strategy Sessions are provided in the book (except for the turnaround exercise, Strategy Session 12). The students are not required to gather additional material. However, where applicable, references to Web sites and other texts are provided for those interested.

We are confident these exercises will add value to your classes as they have done to ours. These exercises have been extensively tested with students and have benefited from student and instructor feedback. We encourage you to contact us with your ideas for clarification or improvement based on your experience. Use the email links at our South-Western authors' Web site at **http://siciliano.swcollege. com** or email us directly at the addresses given below.

Julie I. Siciliano
Western New England College
jsicilia@wnec.edu

C. Gopinath
Suffolk University
cgopinat@acad.suffolk.edu

References

Bandura, A. 1977. *Social Learning Theory.* New York: General Learning Press.

Bonwell, Charles C. and James A. 1991. Active learning: Creating excitement in the classroom. *ASHE-ERIC Higher Education Report No. 1.* Washington, DC: The George Washington University, School of Education and Human Development.

House, R. J. 1982. Experiential Learning: A social learning theory analysis. In *Management Education*, edited by R. D. Freedman, C. L. Cooper, and S. A. Stumpf. New York: John Wiley and Sons.

Siciliano, J. 1999. A template for managing teamwork in courses across the curriculum. *The Journal of Education for Business.* 74(5): 261–264.

Siciliano, J. 2001. How to incorporate learning principles in the classroom: It's more than just putting students in teams. *Journal of Management Education.* 25(1): 8–19.

Contents

S t r a t e g y   S e s s i o n   1

D e c i s i o n   M a k i n g   a t   t h e   S t r a t e g i c   a n d   O p e r a t i o n a l   L e v e l

Exercise: Innkeepers of America

OBJECTIVE

In this session, the concept of strategy is explored by distinguishing it from operational issues.

Time: 20 minutes

ADMINISTRATION

This session's exercise is an excellent opening exercise for the course. On an individual basis, students typically do the reading and identify the decisions as strategic or operational within ten minutes. This can be done during class or before class.

Bring to class an overhead slide of the chart and a marker. Once students have completed the exercise, begin class discussion by putting the chart on the projector and reviewing each of the decisions.

Remind students that one way to distinguish whether a decision is strategic is to consider whether it will alter the company's position in the industry. Sometimes students are unclear about why a decision is operational, especially when it appears to have an effect on profit, when it affects the level of customer service, and so on. To clarify the distinction, use the college or university as an example. (See the discussion for Items 3, 9, 11, and 15 below.)

__S__ 1.   Innkeepers of America's position in the economy segment of the lodging industry.

       This decision identifies the strategic positioning of the company in the industry.

__S__ 2.   Locating properties next to a restaurant rather than have food and beverage in-house.

       This strategic decision drives what type of facility is built and where it is located.

__O__ 3.   Price of rooms lowered further to meet competition.

       This is operational, because the company has already settled on a low price structure, and this decision is not causing a major shift in the organization's pricing policies. Typically, the marketing function is responsible for gauging price sensitivity in the marketplace. (If the pricing decision was to increase prices to rate levels charged by midmarket or first-class/upscale competitors, then one could argue that the decision was more strategic in nature.) An example with

1

which students readily identify is if their college or university were to raise tuition or drop tuition slightly (by 2 or 3%). Would this alter the institution's positioning in terms of the competition?

O 4.   New advertising campaign with discount coupons for weekend stays.

This marketing decision is clearly operational. The campaign is designed to solidify Innkeepers of America's position in the economy segment of this industry.

O 5.   Three new customer service positions.

Adding new customer service positions does not change the company's position or overall strategy. It will enhance customer satisfaction, but in and of itself it will not reposition the firm in the industry.

S/O 6.   Shares of company stock issued for employee bonuses.

Although incentive plans typically are operational in nature, this decision can have strategic implications. One could make a strong argument that this is a strategic decision, particularly if the amount of stock issued to employees is large enough to alter the ownership structure of the organization. On the other hand, if the stock issue is a small percentage of total outstanding stock, this decision will not reposition the firm in the industry, and the decision would be considered operational.

O 7.   Providing continental breakfast in the lobby.

Operational—this added feature is not considered a major change in the organization's direction. This service can be set up with paper cups and paper plates, which helps to keep the cost low.

O 8.   Room service (for continental breakfast only).

Similar to Decision 7, adding room service to deliver continental breakfast is not significant enough to alter the company's position in the industry. An interesting discussion topic is whether this decision is a wise one. Staffing issues become critical. Employees must be "on-call" to deliver the continental breakfast quickly. Dishes and trays are now required, and the properties would have to have storage and cleaning equipment (dishwasher, etc.) for these utensils. The requirement of room service staff and serving equipment makes this decision a costly one.

O 9.   Computerized reservation system.

Some students argue that this decision is strategic. However, it does not alter the fundamental direction of the hotel. Ask students to compare this decision to their own experience at the college or university. If registration for courses can now be made online or is been available online, does that alter the type of college or university they are attending? It clearly results in greater convenience for students, but it does not really change the direction of the academic institution they are attending. What would be a "strategic" computer decision would be if a college decided to switch all classes to an online format such as the University of Phoenix.

_O_ 10.   Training program for front-desk employees.

Operational—this decision is clearly a decision for which the human resource department would be responsible. It is designed to enhance the customer's experience during their stay; however, it does not involve a repositioning of the firm in the industry.

_O_ 11.   Web site where reservations can be booked on line.

Some students may argue that the creation of a Web site is strategic, particularly if no other firms have this particular feature. However, as with most organizations today, Web sites are standard in the industry and can be easily imitated by competitors. In academia as well, Web sites are common for institutions, and application forms can be downloaded and submitted via the Internet.

_S_ 12.   New hotel properties built with additional features to appeal to an upscale market.

New properties with additional features (such as pools, saunas, restaurants, and the like) are a change in the firm's positioning. Ask students whether this strategic decision is a good one, particularly if the company does not create a separate identity for the new properties. Without a separate identity, customers will be confused about the type of hotel they are booking from one location to another. Even with a separate identity, management and the staff may not have the experience or competencies needed to operate successfully in this different segment of the industry.

_S_ 13.   Merger with Economy Lodge, Inc.

Typically, mergers are corporate strategies that result in the creation of a new business.

_S_ 14.   Rewrite mission statement.

Rewriting the mission statement, as described in this case, will be to identify the core purpose of the organization. This is a strategic-level decision, since the mission statement identifies the overall direction of the firm.

_O_ 15.   Contracting cleaning and landscaping services.

Contracting these services does not change the position of this company in the industry and would be considered operational. Most students identify this decision as operational. However, using the college or university example is a good way to end the discussion, and students are clearer about the distinction. (If the college or university they are attending contracts out the landscaping services versus having staff handle the mowing and trimming, it would not change the fundamental purpose and positioning of the institution.)

ASSESSMENT

At the end of class, ask students to complete the assessment form on the following page. It provides feedback so that you can determine if your students understand the point of the exercise. Typical answers to the student assessment form follow.

1. What is meant by "operational decisions?" Use examples to help define this term.

    Operational decisions are those made in specialized areas of the business, such as marketing, finance, human resources, and manufacturing. These do not fundamentally change the purpose or position of the company in the industry. Operational decisions often do not affect the corporation entirely, but rather influence a particular branch or department of the organization. An example would be the operation manager's decision to only have three workers on the front desk during the night hours versus seven during day hours.

2. Why is it important to make a distinction between operational and strategic decision making?

    A problem occurs when management does not make the necessary strategic decisions that provide direction for the firm. The danger of being focused on operational, day-to-day decisions without the guidance that the larger decisions provide is that departmental goal conflict may occur. (For example, the research and development department creates a unique, differentiated product, whereas production is set up to build standard, low-cost items.) In the case, notice how the marketing vice president was focusing on operational issues rather than focusing on the strategic decision to be in the economy segment of the industry. (Build up scale properties so that the company could charge higher room rates to cover costs associated with an advertising campaign targeted at budget conscious travelers.)

    The distinction is also important because, without strategic decisions about overall direction, the company can be caught up periodically shifting positions in the industry. Resources may be wasted, and it is difficult to create core competencies.

    Lastly, focusing on operational performance can result in a firm outperforming competition; however, these improvements are often easily imitated (e.g., Web sites).

3. In the Innkeepers of America case, who specifically was talking about strategic actions? Briefly discuss your answer.

    President—merger with Economy Lodge, Inc., and mission statement revision.

    Operations vice president—new properties be designed with more features to appeal to an upscale market.

Note: The Marketing vice president focused on operational issues (new Web site and higher prices for rooms to cover the ad campaign costs).

Name: _____

ASSESSMENT FORM: DECISION MAKING AT THE STRATEGIC AND OPERATIONAL LEVEL

1. What is meant by "operational decisions?" Use examples to help define this term.

_____

_____

_____

_____

_____

_____

_____

_____

2. Why is it important to make a distinction between operational and strategic decision making?

_____

_____

_____

_____

_____

_____

_____

_____

_____

_____

_____

_____

3. In the Innkeepers of America case, who specifically was talking about strategic actions? Briefly discuss your answer.

_____

_____

_____

_____

_____

Exercise: How Do You Define Strategy?

OBJECTIVE

This session's reading and exercise provide the opportunity to explore strategy from several points of view. It highlights for student the different ways in which the term "strategy" is used, and it illustrates the difference between intentional or planned strategies and those strategies that emerge.

Time: 30 minutes

ADMINISTRATION

If used in a session following Strategy Session 1, this exercise can be completed in 15 minutes, since it involves the same Innkeepers of America case. Allow 15 minutes for the debriefing phase described below. Alternatively, students, on an individual basis before class, can complete the exercise form. Then collect the forms for individual assessment.

DEBRIEFING

In the exercise, students define strategy based on the Innkeepers of America case. They find evidence of the different forms of strategy in the case and then record the evidence according to the form of strategy in the tables contained in the student text, the solution to which is shown in Figure 2.1.

In addition to exploring strategy from several points of view, the concept of Mintzberg's five Ps helps students understand that strategies can "form" in an organization without being consciously intended or planned. According to Mintzberg, if we recognize this, we can pinpoint problem areas and better manage the strategy process within the company's perspective, which is harder to change, as is the personality of individuals. The Innkeepers case is an example of an organization that planned one course of action. However, it actually began to move towards another in line with its perspective of aggressive and reactionary moves. By examining strategy from these different viewpoints, the situation in this case becomes clearer.

The debriefing can center on the following issues:

1. Is the intended strategy working (that is, the strategy as a "plan")?

   The only indication that we have from the case of whether the intended strategy is working is through information pertaining to market share. Market share is dropping and the company is exploring several steps to improve this situation. Therefore, the originally planned or intended strategy does not appear to be working. The question is "why not?"

Figure 2.1 Solution to Exercise: How Do You Define Strategy?

Form of Strategy	Evidence/Actions
Plan	"Management developed a series of steps that they've followed over the past two years." **Discussion:** This suggests management, based on an analysis of the situation at that time, developed a plan that they have been implementing.
Ploy	" . . . lowered the price of hotel rooms by 10% last year and again this year . . ." **Discussion:** Suggests a short-term action by management to meet competition, and this short term action is not really part of a long-term strategy.
Pattern	Several actions of management: (a) breakfast menu with room service, computerized reservation, and (b) dropping prices and discount coupons. **Discussion:** No particular pattern emerges that is a part of the problem faced by the hotel. Actions described as (a) suggests a move into more service and conveniences, while (b) suggests staying in the low end of the industry.
Position	" . . . Innkeepers of America, a medium sized national hotel chain, has operated successfully for many years in the economy segment of the lodging industry. To keep costs low, the company . . . " **Discussion:** The company's position defines where the organization is located in the industry. Innkeepers of America views itself as belonging to the economy segment of the lodging industry, and its market share measures success of this position.
Perspective	"To meet the new competitive threat, management . . . lowered the price of the hotel rooms by 10% . . . created a new advertising campaign . . . three new positions were created and filled in the customer service department . . . Employees were given shares of the company stock . . . continental breakfast menu was created . . . " **Discussion:** The company's "personality" or perspective is aggressive and reactionary in terms of defending its position in the industry. The case discusses the various steps management has undertaken to meet the competitive threat. Other than this, the company does not seem to have a view of itself and what it stands for.

2. How do the different definitions help us to understand the strategy that has begun to "form?"

    We can pinpoint problem areas as we review the different definitions of strategy outlined in Figure 2.1. These definitions have themselves given us an idea that the company lacks a clear view of its position, and this is the reason new courses of action have emerged. In fact, it appears that a new strategy "plan" will be identified once management completes their present deliberations and arrives at another series of steps to be taken. We also see that the new courses of action that have emerged are in line with the company's "personality" or perspective. In an ideal situation, the five Ps would complement each other. When they do not, they provide clues to problems in the formulation and implementation of the strategy.

3. What can the CEO do to manage the process at this time?

    The CEO needs to manage the process so that the Ps are interrelated. For example, the organization's new plan should be in line with the patterns of decisions that are made to support the plan. Again, if a new plan is designed to move the company out of the economy segment, then the decision to merge with Economy Lodge, Inc. would be rejected. The company's aggressive and reactionary behavior must also be monitored to support the repositioning of the company in the industry.

ASSESSMENT

The feedback form for student assessment at the end of this session's notes yields focused responses to very specific questions about the material and its coverage for this and other strategy session classes. Instructors can quickly and easily analyze data from the form and use the results to make timely adjustments in their teaching. Students profit by providing detailed feedback on teaching early enough to benefit from its use. When the results of the class's feedback are shared, instructors can demonstrate their concern with student progress and their willingness to respond to reasonable suggestions.

When this form is used in the early weeks of the class, it can be administered at regular intervals during the semester. The form is best administered during the last five minutes or so of the class, providing more time to analyze and summarize feedback before the next class session.

After the results have been shared with the class, outline the specific action(s) you intend to take in response to student reactions. In carrying out this technique and following up with related adjustments, the instructor provides a role model for students of a professional who is sufficiently self-assured to listen to and learn from his or her students' criticisms, opinions, and insights. Since evaluation is a critical factor in many jobs, students learn to make constructive us of it through the instructor's example.

Note: Don't overuse the feedback form technique (two or perhaps three times at most during the course of a semester).

Name: _____

ASSESSMENT FORM: FOR STUDENTS TO ASSESS THE CLASS AND INSTRUCTOR

Directions: Please respond honestly and constructively to the questions below by circling the response you most agree with in items 1 and 2 and writing brief comments for items 3 and 4.

1. On the scale below, please rate the *clarity* of today's session.

1	2	3	4	5
Totally unclear		Mostly clear		Extremely clear

2. Overall, how *useful* was today's session in helping you learn the material?

1	2	3	4	5
Not useful		Somewhat useful		Extremely useful

3. What did you find most helpful about today's class? (Please list one or two specific examples.)

_____

_____

_____

_____

_____

_____

_____

_____

_____

_____

_____

_____

4. How could the class have been improved? (Please give one or two specific suggestions.)

_____

_____

_____

_____

_____

_____

_____

_____

_____

Strategy Session 3

Communicating Purpose Through Mission Statements

Exercise: How Well Do These Organizations Communicate Their Purpose?

OBJECTIVE

This session shows whether organizations define their core purpose by simply describing current product lines and the services they provide—or whether they define their core purpose in terms of the customers needs being satisfied.

Time: 60–70 minutes

ADMINISTRATION

Process

This strategy session's exercise includes several components: preassessment completed before class; an optional instructor overview of the mission statement criteria; an in-class team activity; and an in-class individual assessment at the end of the exercise.

1. **Reading and Preassessment** Students should complete the reading and the preassessment form before class. The reading provides an overview of the mission statement criteria:

    a. Defining the organization's core purpose in terms of customer needs.
    b. Outlining the organization's philosophy and values. On the preassessment form in the text, students rate how well the mission statements of Harley-Davidson, Continental Airlines, and American United Life Insurance Company meet the suggested criteria.

2. **Optional Instructor's Discussion of Mission Statement Criteria**   (10 minutes) The first criteria—defining the company's purpose in terms of customer needs and not products/services provided—involves a major paradigm shift for many people. It is easier to think of a company's purpose in terms of the products or services it provides, and students at all levels gravitate towards the product/service definition of the business. Therefore, to help students understand the distinction, at the start of class—or at the end of the previous class before students complete the preassessment form—provide a ten-minute overview of the reading. This overview gives other examples of customer need definitions, and is provided in these session notes.

3. **Team Activity**   (35 minutes for work session; 25 minutes for teams to show their ratings and recommended new statements to the class) In class, on the sheet provided in the text, teams of four or five students record all of their individual ratings for each com-

company's mission statement. Through consensus, they develop a new team rating for each of the statements and answer the five questions on the team activity sheet.

Explain to teams that averaging the ratings will not work. For example, if one student gives a particular company a 1 (no core purpose discussed) and another gives the company a 3 (defines core purpose in terms of customer needs), the average of these ratings would be a 2. However, this rating says that the core purpose is defined in terms of a product/service definition, which neither of the team members had designated.

Copy blank team-activity sheets onto overhead transparencies and bring one for each team to class. Teams transfer their information onto the overhead transparency and show the class their final ratings and answers to questions 3, 4, and 5, as time permits.

4. **Individual Assessment**   At the end of the session or at the start of the next class, students complete the individual assessment form included in this instructor's note. The purpose of this individual assessment is to determine whether students understand the mission statement criteria proposition because of the team activity.

Instructor's Overview

To help students understand the difference between product/service-oriented definitions of a company's purpose and the customer-need definitions, begin by telling students that our goal is to fill in the following blank using a customer-needs definition of the business and not a product/service-oriented definition.

We are in the business of _____.

(customer-needs definition)

Then draw the chart in Figure 3.1 on the board to show how the customer-needs definition can be developed from the product/service definition. The first step is to identify the products or services a company provides (the left hand side of the chart). The next step is to answer "Why these products or services are provided" and then place that answer on the right-hand side of the chart.

The examples, shown in Figure 3.1 are given one by one. Our favorites are IBM (when it made "Selectric" Typewriters in the 1970s), XYZ Flower Shop (use one from the area), and ABC Buggy Whip Company (a hypothetical company). These are but a few examples. As the semester progresses, watch for information to reinforce this approach to defining a company's purpose (discussed further in the book *Built to Last* by James C. Collins and Jerry I. Porras and in their *Harvard Business Review* article, "Building your company's vision," September–October 1996, pages 65–77).

For example, Dictaphone Corp. recently changed its vision of a company that produced dictating machines to one that "records, stores and retrieves data that happens to enter the system as voice." With this new definition of its purpose, the company sees expansion into products that will use systems to log, monitor and trace telephone calls to customer help desks, financial trading floors and 911 emergency lines.

One last example about a service organization: At the 25th anniversary of the Pioneer Valley Transit Authority, Massachusetts' largest state transit authority, its Administrator told the audience

Figure 3.1 Customer-Needs Definition from the Product/Service Definition

	Product/Service Definition (*What* product the company makes or, in the case of a service organization, what service it provides.)	**Customer-Needs Definition** (*Why* these products are made or services are provided.)
IBM **in the 1970s**	In the 1970s, IBM produced the most innovative typewriter of its time. The Selectric allowed people to change fonts on their papers by switching a steel golf ball-like device. (Older students remember these and often elaborate on this innovative feature!) The product definition = TYPEWRITERS	To "get to" this side of the chart, ask students why people bought typewriters? The customer-needs definition = TO PROCESS INFORMATION (Further explain that even though IBM is now making other products to satisfy this need—i.e., computers—the customer need definition has not changed, but the product to satisfy that need is virtually obsolete. Companies such as Olivetti and Smith Corona were "left behind" because they continued to think of their purpose as making typewriters.)
XYZ **Flower Shop**	The product = FLOWER ARRANGEMENTS	Why do people buy flower arrangements? The customer needs definition = TO EXPRESS SENTIMENTS Note how this definition helps management to grow while maintaining an overall strategic direction. (That is, "What other products and services can we offer that allow people to express sentiments and emotions?") Students suggest examples such as gifts and cards that fit this strategic purpose.
ABC Buggy **Whip Co.**	You may have to explain what this company made! These were the leather belt-like straps that drivers of carriages—or buggies—used to get the horse that pulled the buggy to go faster. The product = BUGGY WHIPS	Why did people buy these whips? The customer needs definition = FOR VEHICLE ACCELERATION! Use this example for a little humor and explain that ABC Buggy Whip Co. made the best buggy whips on the market (high quality, innovative "snap" feature, etc.) right to the end! However, had they defined their business as vehicle acceleration, they might have moved into products such as gas pedals, and still be around today.

that the PVTA is not just a "bus" company. Instead he described the company's purpose as eliminating transportation as a barrier to what people want to do and where they want to go (carry workers to and from their jobs, assist some in making the transition from welfare to work, help people attend school, see friends and family, go to church, visit museums, libraries, and historic and cultural attractions). On an even broader scale, the company sees its role as decreasing traffic congestion and as an instrument of economic development for the region. Future projects are approved based on their likelihood of implementing the company's expanded mission.

Team Activity Form

Students in teams complete the team activity forms. The following discussions reveal the possible outcomes.

7. Transfer each team member's ratings onto the charts below:

Team Member	Core Purpose			Philosophy and Values		
	Harley-Davidson	Continental Airlines	American United Life	Harley-Davidson	Continental Airlines	American United Life

8. Discuss the above individual ratings. Through consensus, develop a new team rating of a 1, 2, or 3 for each of the mission statements.

Core Purpose			Philosophy and Values		
Harley-Davidson	Continental Airlines	American United Life	Harley-Davidson	Continental Airlines	American United Life

Students typically give American United Life a 3 rating for the core purpose (provide security and peace of mind to our customers) and a 3 rating for the philosophy and values, given that the values are listed in their mission. The Harley-Davidson statement either gets a 2 rating for its core purpose because of the emphasis on motorcycles—the product or a 3 rating because of the statement "we fulfill dreams through the experience . . . ." This is a good opportunity to discuss whether the statement "motorcycles and branded products" is too limiting . . . or does it actually keep the company focused. In this statement there is no discussion of company values or its philosophy about social responsibility. Lastly, the Continental Airlines statement should have a 2 rating given that "to be the best airline" exactly fits the product/service definition. This is very similar to Theodore Levitt's classic discussion of marketing myopia, where the decline of the U. S. railroads during the 1960s resulted in their failure to have a customer-oriented mission by assuming that they were in the railroad business rather than in the transportation business.

9. Rewrite one of the company statements to incorporate an improved definition of the core purpose according to the customer needs criteria.

Most teams will rewrite the Continental Airlines statement from being an airline to providing safe, reliable transportation. Encourage them to also incorporate people's need for quick, speedy transportation that this type of organization can provide that buses and trains do not.

10. Pick one of the company statements that could include more information regarding philosophy and values. Give examples of what might be included.

Students will add information to the Harley-Davidson and Continental Airlines statement about corporate social responsibility in terms of various stakeholders (employees, community, and so on).

11. What other characteristics of the statements did your team notice/discuss?

Some teams will note that they liked the shorter statements better. They are easier to remember and can be reproduced easily onto various company pieces (such as the back of employee business cards, company brochures, stationery, and the like). The one drawback is that when mission statements include only the briefest of information, they are less helpful in serving as a decision-making and leadership tool for operational-level decisions. For example, the strong orientation to partnerships with customers that American United Life Insurance Company emphasizes would provide guidance to management in reviewing various programs and policies. This type of information would not be available to Continental Airlines' management.

ASSESSMENT

Ask students to complete the individual assessment following page 20 after the exercise is complete.

Answers to Assessment

Company	Product/Service Definition Of the Company's Business/ Core Purpose	Customer Needs Definition of the Company's Business/ Core Purpose
Apple Computer	Computers	Store, process, retrieve information
YMCA	Work-out/exercise sessions Swimming classes Day care facilities	Help people to build body, spirit, and mind
XYX Furnace Cleaning Co.	Clean dust from furnace Oil parts Vacuum furnace ducts	Provide a clean and healthy home and office environment

1. Why is the customer needs version more difficult to write?

    It is more difficult to write because the customer needs definition is less obvious, less tangible. The product/service definition describes simply what the company does or provides.

2. What might happen if decision makers focus primarily on the product/service definition of the company's business as its core purpose?

    Two things can happen if decision makers think of the company's purpose solely in terms of the product or service it provides. First, individuals in the company can become myopic when it comes to new technologies. They do not consider the new technologies as part of "our business." The typewriter example is a good one. Thinking that "typewriters" were their business caused companies like Olivetti to become too focused on outdated technology. Theodore Leavitt's classic example of the railroad industry is another example.

    Second, management has little direction for growth into new products and services or for assistance in making operational-level decisions. The furnace cleaning company is a good example of how the revised definition of the company's purpose provides direction for expanding into new products and services. One of our adult learners owned this type of business. He wanted to grow but was unsure of the direction. This exercise provided him with a clearer vision of his company's purpose, and he decided to offer a new line of products, such as scented air filters, blowers to enhance air flow, etc., that enhanced the home and office environment. Examples of how the customer-needs definition provides assistance in making operational-level decisions are given in the reading to this strategy session (fire station and AT&T).

3. What is the benefit of including information about the company's philosophy and values?

    This aspect of the mission statement provides guidelines for those within the company, particularly in terms of behavior . . . their conduct and how they conduct business. The Johnson & Johnson Credo proved to be the classic example of guiding important decisions during the Tylenol crisis. Its Credo articulates the belief that the company's first responsibility is to the doctors, nurses, and patients who use its product, followed by the employees, communities in which employees live and work, and finally the company's shareholders. By taking actions consistent with its values and philosophy, J&J presented itself as a company that was willing to do what was right for its customers regardless of the cost to shareholders.

Name:_____

ASSESSMENT FORM

Directions: On the chart below, write a definition of the core purpose of each company from a product/service perspective and then from a customer needs perspective. Then answer questions 1 through 3 that follow.

Company	Product/Service Definition Of the Company's Business/ Core Purpose	Customer Needs Definition of the Company's Business/ Core Purpose
Apple Computer		
YMCA		
XYX Furnace Cleaning Co.		

1. Why is the customer needs version more difficult to write?

_____

_____

_____

_____

_____

_____

2. What might happen if decision makers focus primarily on the product/service definition of the company's business as its core purpose?

_____

_____

_____

_____

_____

3. What is the benefit of including information about the company's philosophy and values?

_____

_____

_____

_____

_____

The Board's Role in Corporate Governance

Exercise: Translating the Board's Role into Guidelines for Practice

OBJECTIVE

This session helps students understand the different roles of a Board of Directors and how these roles affect the way a Board operates. Normally, the strategic management course focuses on the role of the CEO. However, the Board of Directors has important roles to play and an understanding of these roles is necessary to understanding the corporation as a whole.

Time: 75 minutes

ADMINISTRATION

Individual or Team Activity

This exercise can be an individual or team activity for two or three participants.

Completing the Guidelines (25 minutes)

There are two parts to this exercise. Instruct the students to do Part I first—that is, discuss the guidelines one at a time and identify the appropriate role or roles of the Board reflected in each numbered guideline. Let students stop after the guidelines for a discussion before they complete Part II, in which they consider the Disney Board.

Discussion (30 minutes)

This set of guidelines is a path-breaking effort on the part of a U.S. company. Boards are reluctant to impose any set of restrictions or guidelines for themselves, and the fact that this was done by one of the largest companies in the world is notable. These guidelines were developed after a particularly bad time in the history of GM's corporate governance. In the early 1990s, the company's performance was causing concern. After great effort, the Board managed to oust the controversial Chairman and CEO Roger Smith as it was felt that there was need for new leadership to address the problems faced by GM. In light of that experience, these guidelines were developed with the active involvement of the outside directors to see that the situation did not repeat itself.

The Board has adopted twenty-eight guidelines. For this exercise, the students are provided with an abridged version of them. On the face of it, these guidelines may appear to be simple matters of housekeeping. However, the process of assigning roles in these guidelines will make the students realize the implications of each guideline as explained further in the suggested outcomes of discussion below. After the students assign roles to the items, the debriefing can begin. The instructor can take up the discussion of the first three items, and then call for student teams to comment on items that are of particular interest to them.

Selection and Composition of the Board

1. *Board Membership Criteria* (**Control, Service, and Strategy**)

2. *Selection and Orientation of New Directors* (**Control, Service, and Strategy**)

These two items deal with membership of the Board. In selecting members carefully, the Board can ensure that it has sufficient representation of skills for its service role and for its strategy role, apart from control. By requiring the invitation for new members to come from the Board and not just the CEO, the guidelines try to ensure the loyalty of the directors be to the entire Board and the company, and not be focused on the CEO. Traditionally, directors were considered to have been selected by the CEO and thus personally loyal to him.

Board Leadership

3. *Selection of Chairman and CEO* (**Control**)

Meeting Procedures

12. *Selection of Agenda Items for Board Meetings* (**Control**)

When the Chairman and CEO are the same person, there is an enormous concentration of power in the hands of one person. Some corporate governance specialists believe that the two positions must be separated and the Chairman must be an independent director. These guidelines have left this issue open. However, the instructor can explain to students that elsewhere in the guidelines—not included in the version reproduced in their student text—the objective of trimming the power of the Chairman has been achieved by stipulating that when the Chairman and CEO are the same person, the Chairman of the powerful Executive Committee needs to be an independent director.

The power of the Chairman is derived from his or her ability to set the agenda (Item 12) for the meeting, much like the power of the Speaker of the House of Representatives). GM has dealt with the concentration of power issue by also giving the CEO input into the agenda.

Board Composition and Performance

4. *Mix of Management and Independent Directors* (**Control and Strategy**)

5. *Board Definition of What Constitutes Independence for Directors* (**Control and Strategy**)

A greater number of outside directors on the Board ensures a level of independence of behavior that helps in control. It can also contribute to strategy since the independent (i.e., outside) directors bring non-GM perspectives to the enterprise. Unlike General Motors, many firms are not prepared to take a firm stand that outside members should make a majority. The Board has also taken the unusual step of defining what it considers independence.

6. *Former Chief Executive Officer's Board Membership* **(Control and Strategy)**

The former CEO can bring continuity to the operations of the company and can therefore play a useful role. However, he or she may serve as a constraint if the Board wishes to revisit past decisions and making changes in strategy.

7. *Directors Who Change Their Present Job Responsibility* **(Control, Service, and Strategy)**

8. *Term Limits* **(Control, Service, and Strategy)**

The Board is also trying to ensure its effectiveness by allowing for the removal of older members, and those whose connections have changed. This enables the Board to keep its skills current and relevant for the three roles it needs to play. The issue of term limits is similar to the general debate in society about term limits for representatives in local, state, and federal legislative bodies.

9. *Assessing the Board's Performance* **(Control, Service, and Strategy)**

It is highly unusual in corporate governance for a board to review its own performance. This guideline forces the GM Board to undertake self-evaluation and keep itself current by reviewing membership and its contribution to the company.

10. *Interaction with Institutional Investors, Press, Customers, etc.* **(Service)**

This is the only place where the Board recognizes the importance of stakeholders and the need to communicate with them. The Board is willing to play a role here but at management's request. This will ensure that the company speaks with one voice to the external interests.

Board Relationship to Senior Management

11. *Board Access to Senior Management* **(Control and Strategy)**

Meeting Procedures

13. *Board Materials Distributed in Advance* **(Control and Strategy)**

These deal with access to information and interaction between the Board and management. By allowing senior management to attend Board meetings and to participate, the directors have the opportunity to engage in direct discussions with them and give them the opportunity to understand the Board's thinking without always being filtered through the CEO. CEOs are sometimes uncomfortable with director's talking directly with management personnel. Apart from diluting the Chairman's control of information provided to the Board, such contacts between Directors and managerial personnel can distract the latter in their day-to-day operations.

    If the CEO wishes to control the directors' knowledge of operations and organizational details, not sending sufficient information, not sending it in a timely fashion, or sending too much information can be an undesirable tactic. Item 16 directly addresses this issue.

Committee Matters

14. *Number, Structure, and Independence of Committees* **(Control and Strategy)**

A board works through its committees, which meet more often than the full board. Decisions taken by the committees are ratified by the full board.

Leadership Development

15. *Formal Evaluation of the Chief Executive Officer* **(Control and Strategy)**

This item goes to the heart of the control issue. Boards have often accused of being soft on the CEO. This guideline sets up a formal review system, and specifically includes the issue of strategy for evaluation. It also addresses the important issue of CEO compensation by tying it to evaluation on objective criteria.

Open-Ended Question   Students may notice that most of the items deal with control, which is the traditional role of the Board. Their role in strategy is still emerging and debatable and is left to the initiative of the individuals of the Board. The students are asked to identify some items they would want included in the guidelines. These could include:

1. The Board needs to set for itself a mission so that all members of the Board would be aware of what is expected of them;
2. There should be one session of the full Board in a year when the strategy of the company would be explicitly discussed (as different from reviewing the performance and approving the annual report);
3. A Committee on Strategy could be formed that would exclusively deal with issues pertaining to overseeing the strategy of the firm; and
4. A mission and specific goals are set for each committee of the Board and are shared with all members.

Evaluating Disney Board (20 minutes)

The instructor may now ask the team to evaluate the Disney Board in the light of the foregoing discussion. About 10 minutes can be allotted for this. In the discussion that follows, which can take about 10 minutes, too, the students will immediately raise the following issues:

1. *The lack of independence of some members owing to their pecuniary connections with the company or to Eisner in person.* There are clear conflicts of interest in the case of several members. Specifically, Bowers is the head of the school where Eisner's children attended classes. Gold manages investments for the Disney family. Mitchell received payment from the company for consulting services. O'Donovan is president of Georgetown University, where one of Eisner's children attended college. Russell is Eisner's lawyer. Stern is an architect who designed Disney projects. Walker participated in a company incentive plan. (This situation in Disney violates GM's guideline 5).
2. *The possible contribution of the members to the Board's roles.* It could be pointed out that Sidney Poitier, although "just" an actor, brings a critical perspective to an entertainment com-

pany. Similarly, although Ms. Bowers' position appears to be due to her personal connection, she is probably an educationist whose views are important since children are an important customer segment for Disney.

At the time, Disney replied to charges of conflict of interest in the composition of its Board with the defense that company's performance was good. For that reason, there was no need to be concerned with the company's governance. However, Disney's profits after 1996 declined, as discussed in Strategy Session 9. In addition, the Board's strategy role is to position the company for the future and is not meant to reflect or explain current performance

ASSESSMENT

Ask students to complete the individual assessment following page 28 after the exercise is complete. Possible answers to the questions follow.

Answers to Assessment

1. Does the Chief Executive Officer of an organization answer to anyone? (circle one)

    Yes   **No**

   If yes, to whom does the CEO answer? **The CEO answers to the Board**

2. Which role of the Board ensures that the Management operates in the best interest of the owners of the company?

   Answer: Control, since it is an internally focused role. Control means the Board serves as a watchdog over management—monitoring the competence of the management group and overseeing resource allocation.

3. Describe any two of the guidelines that would help the Board in its Strategy role.

   Answer: 15, Formal Evaluation of the Chief Executive Officer, since this guideline includes reviewing the CEO's accomplishment of long-term strategic objectives. 11, Evaluation of the Board's Performance, since this guideline includes an assessment of the Board's contribution—which would include a criteria for Board involvement in setting or approving strategic direction; and 14, Access to Senior Management for Information, since this guideline enables the Board to get information about how the management team is dealing with strategic issues.

4. What arguments can GM's Management present to argue against the Board's involvement in strategy through setting up a separate committee for the purpose?

   Answer: The Board's control role gives it enough authority to evaluate performance and thus judge if the strategy is working. A separate committee would be distracting to senior management, who have the responsibility for strategy, and this committee introduces an additional layer that is not necessary. In addition, some scholars argue that the involvement in strategy should be each Board member's responsibility, since it deals with the overall direction of the company. The argument suggests it should not just be the primary responsibility of a separate committee.)

Name: _____

ASSESSMENT FORM: STRATEGY SESSION 4

Directions: Answer the questions on the form below.

1. Does the Chief Executive Officer of an organization answer to anyone? (Circle one.)

    Yes   No

    If yes, to whom does the CEO answer? _____

2. Which role of the Board ensures that the Management operates in the best interest of the owners of the company?

    _____

    _____

    _____

    _____

    _____

    _____

3. Describe any two of the guidelines that would help the Board in its Strategy role.

    _____

    _____

    _____

    _____

4. What arguments can GM's Management present to argue against the Board's involvement in strategy through setting up a separate Committee for the purpose?

S t r a t e g y   S e s s i o n   5

V i e w i n g   S t r a t e g y   f r o m   t h e   S t a k e h o l d e r
P e r s p e c t i v e

Exercise: Role Playing Microsoft Corporation
Stakeholder Interests and Power

OBJECTIVE

In this session, students view the interests and power of various stakeholder groups that management must take into account when formulating strategy

TIME: 75 minutes

ADMINISTRATION

This exercise involves four rounds of meetings:

1. Students meet in stakeholder groups to discuss the case and develop their positions.
2. The class reconvenes to hear the Microsoft strategy and the stakeholders' brief response to the strategy.
3. The groups meet to discuss any modifications as a result of the strategy.
4. The class reconvenes to hear any changes.

Instructions

1. **Introduction** (10 minutes)   The instructor introduces the exercise by briefly reviewing the Microsoft case. The specific setting in which the groups meet is described. The top-management stakeholder team is expected to provide the outline of a strategic plan for the next three years that assures Microsoft Corporation of continued profitability and growth. It must develop its plan either based on keeping the organization intact—or breaking up the corporation into separate company structures.

    Note: This case was chosen because it involves a well-known company and because this case deals with options (breakup the company or leave it as is) that students clearly understand. Because the case is a "situation in progress," there will be court cases, appeals, and, perhaps changes in government policy. Updates are available on the home page for instructors. However, it is important to reinforce to students that the primary purpose of this exercise is to understand the impact different stakeholders have on strategy, and this exercise still serves that purpose.

    It is important that students have read the case thoroughly and have either been assigned to one of the various stakeholder groups or are aware of the variety of groups in which they may be placed for the exercise. The preassessment form is included to ensure student reading before class.

2. **Divide Class into Stakeholders** (5 minutes)   The class is divided into six groups:
   a. Microsoft top management
   b. Microsoft stockholders
   c. Government—i.e., the Justice Department
   d. Executives from competitors such as Netscape, AOL, Apple, and Compaq
   e. Suppliers such as Intel
   f. Microsoft employees

   Depending on the size of the class and the way in which the instructor wants to guide the discussion, the number of groups can be expanded or contracted. A class of 30 may have five students in each group, or if the instructor wants to emphasize the role of the competitors, for example, these could be designated separately—one group Netscape and AOL, another group Apple and Compaq.

   Instructions for group discussion are reproduced at the end of this session's notes and should be distributed as guidelines for preparation. A time limit of about five to seven minutes is allotted for reading the guidelines and setting up the group.

3. **Stakeholder discussions** (30 minutes)   The stakeholder groups meet to discuss the case and develop their specific positions on what the Microsoft strategy should be while management formulates its strategic plan.

   Each stakeholder group should select one person to act as spokesperson—and the team that comprises the management stakeholder group should divide responsibilities among its various members. These instructions are given in the guidelines discussed in item 2—that is, product/marketing, operations, human resources, and so on.

4. **Stakeholder groups meet together** (40–45 minutes)   The entire class reconvenes with each stakeholder group staying intact. The Microsoft management team presents its plan and answers any questions of clarification. Then the stakeholder groups huddle individually for five minutes to review their positions in light of the Microsoft presentation.

   A spokesperson from each group gives a brief response to the strategic plan. The management team in turn is allowed to respond in a very brief manner. Once all of the stakeholder groups have presented, a question and answer period directed to the management team is in order.

5. **Second round of stakeholder discussions** (10 minutes)   A second brief round of meetings takes place. Microsoft's management team should reassess its strategic plan in light of the critiques by various groups. Each stakeholder group should discuss its position in relationship to the corporation as well as other stakeholder groups.

6. **Stakeholders meet again** (10–15 minutes)   The entire class reconvenes. Microsoft management presents any changes in its strategic plan. Each stakeholder is given an opportunity to make a brief statement.

MICROSOFT CASE: PREASSESSMENT

Ideal student responses for the preassessment form that ensures that students have read and understand the Microsoft case follow.

1. After reading the case U. S. versus Microsoft Corporation, what strategy should Microsoft pursue at this time and why?

This question is designed to get the students to think of strategic options for Microsoft. Some students may suggest that Microsoft should breakup the company, since this may be one inevitable outcome, particularly if Microsoft loses the appeal. In addition, some students may argue that the breakup of Microsoft could be a blessing in disguise for Gates and Ballmer. Computing now means the Internet. Much of the time at a PC is devoted to Internet activities. Windows became powerful because it was the standard for personal computing. With the growing importance of Web delivery and the customization that it allows, the relative importance of operating systems and the applications that it supports will change.

2. Identify as many stakeholders of Microsoft Corporation as you can. List them according to the level of influence they exert over the company, showing the stakeholder with the highest level first, then the stakeholder with the next highest level of influence, and so on. The last stakeholder on the list should be the one with the lowest level of influence.

The order of importance may vary; however, typically the stakeholders with the most influence are (1) the government (i.e., the Justice Department); (2) Microsoft top management; (3) Microsoft stockholders; (4) executives from competitors such as Netscape, AOL, Apple, and Compaq; (5) suppliers such as Intel; and lastly (6) Microsoft employees.

TEAM ACTIVITY: STAKEHOLDER GROUPS

Desired outcomes for the end-of-class discussion are suggested below.

1. Did the Microsoft strategic plan have a high probability of success in meeting its corporate goals for the next three years?

Some argue that the breakup of Microsoft could be a blessing in disguise for Gates and Ballmer. Computing now means the Internet. Much of the time at a PC is devoted to Internet activities. Windows became powerful because it was the standard for personal computing. Now the Web is becoming the standard. In a couple of years, no one will care about the operating system.

The true test of Microsoft's future will come with further development of a variety of Web technologies, such as wireless Net access. Has the management team considered this is their strategic plan? How have they handled the breakup ordered by Judge Jackson: by (a) ignoring it because of their confidence in the appeals process; or (b) by beginning to prepare for it?

2. Is stakeholder awareness evident in the plan?

How has the company taken into account the interests and power of the key stakeholder groups? Who are the key stakeholder groups? Clearly, the government and investors have high levels of interest in the company's future direction.

The government also has substantial influence, given the antitrust case. Competitors could become an important ally for the government, since the sanctions require that the two Microsoft companies cannot provide technical information to each other that is not simultaneously made available to other companies.

ASSESSMENT: THE MINUTE PAPER

The purpose of the "minute paper" is to collect written feedback on student learning. To use the minute paper, stop the class two or three minutes early. The following suggested questions:

- Rank order Microsoft stakeholders by level of influence.
- In the class role-playing exercise, which group was the most convincing? Explain why.

provide useful information in two areas:

- First, you can compare student responses regarding the level of influence of stakeholders before and after the exercise—that is, the second question on the preassessment form compared to the first question on this form.
- Second, you can receive feedback from students regarding their impression of the most convincing group. It might be that one group received better information in the instructions. Or, perhaps, another group developed a process that might be worth incorporating on future instructions to group members.

Name: _____

ASSESSMENT FORM: STRATEGY SESSION 5

Directions: Answer the "minute paper" questions on the form below.

1. Rank order Microsoft stakeholders by level of influence.

_____

_____

_____

_____

_____

2. In the class role-playing exercise, which group was the most convincing? Explain why.

_____

_____

_____

_____

_____

_____

Instructions for Stakeholder Group Discussion

MICROSOFT MANAGEMENT TEAM

You are the top management team of Microsoft charged with developing a strategy for the company. Time allowed: 5 to 7 minutes.

1. Review the key aspects of the case.
2. Determine the characteristics of a successful strategy to keep the company profitable and at the forefront of innovation. What are company goals over the next three years?
   a. Work out a product strategy. For example, no longer dictate what Internet content appears on the Windows desktop or market products a la carte (no bundling). After all, Windows was important in the past because it was the standard for personal computing. Now the Web itself is becoming the standard. Make the operating system public property (reveal the code that makes up Windows).
   b. Identify innovations that will keep the company at the forefront of information technology, such as a focus on the Next Generation Windows Services that will be a protected, pervasive network architecture—a computer instruction language that the company could dominate the Internet with in the same way it has ruled the desktop with Windows.
   c. Discuss potential joint ventures and/or acquisitions.
   d. Discuss the company breakup into two entities: an operating-systems company and an applications company.
   e. Work out a human resource strategy that ensures high levels of productivity in the work force.
3. Think through the implications for the various stakeholder groups who will hear your plan. Who will be your allies? Your adversaries? What interests do they have in Microsoft? What kind of power or influence do they have to affect your strategy?
4. Divide up the task of making the presentation with one person acting as Bill Gates, one person acting as the new CEO Steve Ballmer, and the other Executive Vice Presidents in charge of marketing, technology, and human resource management.
5. Work up a brief but persuasive presentation.

MICROSOFT STOCKHOLDERS

You represent all of the Microsoft stockholders, namely individuals who own stock, pension funds, and the like. You are interested in the continued high yields of the corporation. Time allowed: 5 to 7 minutes.

1. Review the key aspects of the case.
2. Identify the interests you have in seeing Microsoft continue as a strong company with high-yield stock.
   a. Focus on the overall strengths and weaknesses of Microsoft as a single corporation versus two separate entities (operating-systems company and applications company).
   b. Discuss the implications of the breakup on share value.
   c. Think about the future of the corporation in light of your desire to increase stockholder wealth.
   d. Review the management changes (Gates and Ballmer) and the implications for future company success.
3. Anticipate the Microsoft management strategic plan in the areas of product strategy—for example, no longer dictate what appears on the Windows desktop; market products a la carte–(no bundling); make the operating system public property; develop new innovations to keep the company at the forefront of information technology; implement human resource strategies to keep employees productive.
4. Identify the other stakeholders who have similar interests and those with different interests.
5. Choose a spokesperson to present your group's perspective when called upon.

FEDERAL GOVERNMENT

You represent the federal government, in particular the Department of Justice (antitrust violations). Time allowed: 5 to 7 minutes.

1. Review the key aspects of the case.
2. Identify the interests you have in seeing Microsoft follow legal guidelines in terms of competitive behavior.
   a. Focus on the role you will play and how you will monitor the company's actions.
   b. Review the impact of the court case on the public and the media.
   c. Think about your bargaining power in light of the court case and how this affects future work at the Department of Justice's antitrust division.
   d. Identify the interests in various publics you represent in ensuring that Microsoft follows legal guidelines.
3. Anticipate the Microsoft management strategic plan in the areas of product strategy—for example, no longer dictate what appears on the Windows desktop; market products a la carte–(no bundling); focus on the Next Generation Windows Services that will be a protected, pervasive network architecture—that is, a computer instruction language with which the company could dominate the Internet in the same way it has ruled the desktop with Windows; make the operating system public property; develop new innovations to keep the company at the forefront of information technology; implement human resource strategies to keep employees productive.
4. Identify the other stakeholders who have similar interests and those with different interests.
5. Choose a spokesperson to present your group's perspective when called upon.

COMPETITORS SUCH AS NETSCAPE, AOL, APPLE, COMPAQ

You represent the management teams of the two major competitors of Microsoft – Netscape and AOL. You have an interest in protecting your market share in the midst of an uncertain future for the industry. Time allowed: 5 to 7 minutes.

1. Review the key aspects of the case.
2. Identify the interests you have in seeing whether Microsoft maintains its competitive clout over the next three years.
   a. Focus on the overall strengths and weaknesses of Microsoft as a competitor.
   b. Discuss the changing character of the market for computers and the role of the Internet.
   c. Discuss the role of the government, particularly given the Microsoft case.
   d. Identify the interests of the various stakeholders of your corporations.
3. Anticipate the Microsoft management strategic plan in the areas of product strategy—for example, no longer dictate what appears on the Windows desktop; market products a la carte–(no bundling); focus on the Next Generation Windows Services that will be a protected, pervasive network architecture—that is, a computer instruction language with which the company could dominate the Internet in the same way it has ruled the desktop with Windows; make the operating system public property; develop new innovations to keep the company at the forefront of information technology; implement human resource strategies to keep employees productive. How would you like to have these formulated to meet your interests or objectives?
4. Identify the other stakeholders who have similar interests and those with different interests.
5. Choose a spokesperson to present your group's perspective when called upon.

MICROSOFT EMPLOYEES

You represent the employees at Microsoft. Your power and interests are more internally focused than some of the other stakeholder groups. Time allowed: 5 to 7 minutes.

1. Review the key aspects of the case.
2. Identify the interests you have in seeing whether Microsoft maintains its market position over the next three years.
   a. Focus on the overall strengths and weaknesses of Microsoft as a competitor.
   b. Discuss trends in the labor market, particular for software organizations.
   c. What role will the Internet play?
   d. Discuss the role of the government, particularly given the Microsoft case.
   e. Identify the interests of the various stakeholders of Microsoft.
3. Anticipate the Microsoft management strategic plan in the areas of product strategy—for example, no longer dictate what appears on the Windows desktop; market products a la carte–(no bundling); focus on the Next Generation Windows Services that will be a protected, pervasive network architecture—that is, a computer instruction language with which the company could dominate the Internet in the same way it has ruled the desktop with Windows; make the operating system public property; develop new innovations to keep the company at the forefront of information technology; implement human resource strategies to keep employees productive.
4. Identify the other stakeholders who will have similar interests and those with different interests.
5. Choose a spokesperson to present your group's perspective when called upon.

MICROSOFT SUPPLIERS

You represent the suppliers to Microsoft, particularly Intel. You are interested in Microsoft's continued growth and success and in having a share of that. Time allowed: 5 to 7 minutes.

1. Review the key aspects of the case.
2. Identify the interests you have in seeing whether Microsoft maintains its market position over the next three years.
   a. Focus on the overall strengths and weaknesses of Microsoft as a competitor.
   b. Discuss trends in the supplier market.
   c. Discuss the role of the government, particularly given the Microsoft case.
   d. Identify the interests of the various stakeholders of Microsoft.
3. Anticipate the Microsoft management strategic plan in the areas of product strategy—for example, no longer dictate what appears on the Windows desktop; market products a la carte–(no bundling); focus on the Next Generation Windows Services that will be a protected, pervasive network architecture—that is, a computer instruction language with which the company could dominate the Internet in the same way it has ruled the desktop with Windows; make the operating system public property; develop new innovations to keep the company at the forefront of information technology.
4. Identify the other stakeholders who will have similar interests to yours and those with different interests.
5. Choose a spokesperson to present your group's perspective when called upon.

Exercise: Intensity of Competition in the Gaming Industry

OBJECTIVE

This session helps students identify the forces of competition and determine what effects these forces have on a competitor's ability to earn high profits.

Time: 20 to 40 minutes

ADMINISTRATION

Students should read the gaming industry case in the exercise and answer the seven questions before coming to class. The answer forms in the student text can be collected from students at the start of the session to quickly assess level of preparation—or returned at the start of the next class if a grading component is associated with this "preassessment."

Instructors may vary the format of the exercise depending on time constraints:

1. **Optional team assignment**   If the instructor chooses a team format, allocate approximately 20 minutes for students to agree upon a group rating for the intensity levels of each force of competition and a response to the parts in Question 7.

2. **Class discussion format**   If a class discussion format is chosen, either with or without the team assignment, the instructor reviews the forces of competition and Question 7 with the entire class, allocating approximately 20 minutes for the discussion. Write the three categories on the board (Low—Medium—High) and, starting with the first force of rivalry among competitors, ask students to raise their hands to indicate their position. Put the score on the board (number in each category). Then discuss the force with the class and get a consensus. Do the same with all of the forces. This provides an overview of the intensity of competition in the industry—and a discussion of the implications of this level of intensity (Question 7) ends the exercise.

IDENTIFYING THE INTENSITY OF EACH OF THE FORCES OF COMPETITION

Correct student responses are underlined below, followed by the possible answers to the questions.

3. Rivalry Among Existing Firms   **High   Medium   Low**

   a)   Define the gaming industry.

   Organizations that provide consumers with access to legal gambling such as dog and horse racetracks, state lotteries, casinos, legal bookmaking operations, card rooms, and Indian reservations.

b) What is its level of concentration?

First, casinos make up the majority of revenues in the industry. To determine the level of concentration, one can look at the amount of casino consolidation that has occurred over the past several years and the ease of entering and exiting the industry (mobility barriers). More firms are merging, which increases the market share held by a few firms. Although there are many casinos, five to six large chains hold the majority of the market share. In addition, mobility barriers are high (cost of entering the industry through construction of casinos, brand names, and the like) and have increased as the industry has matured. As a result, rivalry among existing firms is medium, and firms in the industry, particularly the five to six large chains, enjoy above-average profitability.

4. Bargaining Power of Suppliers   **High   Medium   Low**

a) Who are the suppliers?

Suppliers to casino companies are primarily gambling equipment manufacturers. Labor is also recognized as a supplier, and one that exerts a lot of power in many industries. Also included in this category are other equipment suppliers, such as those who sell televisions that are placed around the casinos, those who supply coin-counting machines, those who sell furniture, and the like. Entertainers are another source of supply, and depending on their popularity, have various levels of bargaining power.

b) Discuss bargaining power.

The tactics of International Game Technology (IGT) in giving away accounting software in exchange for high levels of casino business suggest that gambling equipment manufacturers have had strong bargaining power over the competitors in this industry. However, competitors are beginning to develop high technology video slot machines that differentiate their products from that of long-time suppliers to the industry. If the lawsuit weakens the hold of IGT, the gambling equipment industry could see new entrants. Regarding the labor force, in this industry it does not consist of highly skilled employees or tightly unionized labor that can bargain away a significant amount of profits. Therefore, the level of bargaining power is low for this group. Lastly, because other suppliers, as mentioned above, are numerous, casinos can switch from supplier to supplier relatively easy since switching costs are low. For this reason, the bargaining power of this group is low.

5. Bargaining Power of Buyers   **High   Medium   Low**

a) Who are the buyers?

In this industry, the buyers are the end consumers.

b) Discuss whether they have bargaining power.

Consumer bargaining power is stronger when consumers are purchasing products that are undifferentiated, expensive relative to their incomes, or of a sort where quality is not particularly important to them. Since most of the casinos are differentiated and consumers on average tend to spend entertainment dollars on casino gambling—that is, not significant portions of their income, the bargaining power of buyers would be low.

6. Relative Power of Other Stakeholders   **High** Medium Low

Who are other major stakeholders?

State governments are other stakeholders with strong influence over the industry. Overall, states have limited the expansion of new markets for this industry by not approving gambling in many new territories. The absence of legislative approvals is partly due to the strong U.S. economy, which alleviates the pressure to encourage gaming development as a prospective source of taxes, tourism, and jobs. In addition, it reflects societal concerns about issues of compulsive gambling and the potential problems that the introduction of legalized gaming can bring or aggravate. However, state approvals are not at a standstill, as evidenced by the November 1996 referendum for three casinos in Detroit, the first of which was opened in July 1999. Religious groups, and the like, who are morally opposed to gambling, are also influential in putting pressure on local authorities to prevent casinos from operating.

7. Threat of New Entrants   High **Medium** Low

What are the barriers to entry into this industry?

The primary barrier to entry into this industry is state government licensing requirements. To become a major player in the industry requires large sums of capital. The high profile of some of the existing players in the industry and their influence may also deter newcomers who are wary of challenging established brands. In addition, it used to be said for many years that one of the largest contributors to campaigns to prevent the spread of gambling were the existing gambling companies!

8. Threat of Substitutes   High Medium **Low**

What other substitutes limit the sales and profits for firms in this industry?

Initially, Internet gambling appeared to be one of the largest threats to this industry. It is a substitute if the industry is defined as "casino gambling." The decentralized nature of the Internet and its global reach make it virtually impossible for it to be controlled or deterred by regulation. Legislation is unlikely to end such activity, and even if prohibitions are put in place, full enforcement is difficult, particularly if the sites are foreign-based ("off-shore"). Without access to records of Internet site usage, it will be difficult for law enforcement officials to know who is placing bets and how much they are wagering. It is unlikely that public and government leaders will give a high priority to policing and prosecuting offenders. So while this appears to be a favorable trend for this substitute form of gambling, the remoteness of betting through a personal computer, plus concerns about legality, security, and obtaining winnings will keep many traditional casino visitors from spending much time wagering in cyberspace.

Several states are expanding their lotteries schemes by bringing in new games and aligning with neighboring states to offer large jackpots. These are substitutes for the small-time and occasional gambler. In addition, different forms of sports betting (e.g., horse racing, dog racing, team sports betting) are substitutes, as are illegal numbers games. In the state of Delaware, the local horse racing venue won approval from the state for a limited extension into slot machines only, as a form of challenging the large numbers of people who went to nearby Atlantic City.

9. Now that you have analyzed each of the forces of competition, discuss the implications of the above levels of intensity.

a) Which forces of competition are most threatening now? Which do you expect will change over the next, say, five years?

The most threatening force of competition is the relative power of other stakeholders, namely state governments. Their ability to influence casino operations and expansion is high. The factors that are changing the most are the threat of substitutes (particularly Internet gambling). Because of the decentralized nature of the Internet and its global reach, it is difficult for state governments to exert the type of influence they do on casinos. However, the issues associated with Internet gambling (described above in Item 6) keep this force of competition from being very threatening over the next few years.

b) What are the implications in terms of profit margins in this industry today? Over the next five years?

As noted above, because the industry is consolidating and becoming more concentrated, firms enjoy above-average profitability.

c) As the CEO of a firm in this industry, what actions does this analysis suggest you implement in order to strengthen your competitive strategy?

First, given the strong relative power of state governments, the CEO of a firm can proactively look for ways to benefit the firm's position. This might involve lobbying efforts to influence regulation. Next, given the more mature nature of this industry (evidenced by increased consolidation), positive action can be taken to improve costs internally through tighter budgeting, stricter control, and new performance-based incentive systems for employees. Externally, the costs of purchasing from suppliers rated as having a medium amount of power can be lowered and the bargaining power of the firm improved. Strategies to achieve this involve spreading purchases among alternate suppliers, avoiding switching costs by becoming too dependent on a supplier, or encouraging alternate sources to enter the industry through funding development contracts and contracts for a small part of purchases.

d) As an advisor to a potential entrant, would you recommend entry? What steps would you advise them to take?

Because of the slowdown in gaming approvals in new states, the success of potential entrants relies on entering developed locations, such as Las Vegas and Atlantic City. If internal development is chosen such as building a casino, steps such as offering a superior product or discovering a new niche would be important entry strategies. On the other hand, joint ventures or the buyout of existing firms is another form of entry. In this case, finding a way to operate the casino at a lower cost than current competitors would also help to overcome entry barriers.

ASSESSMENT

At the end of the class, hand out the assessment form at the end of this session's notes. It presents to your students the following problem:

You have a maximum of $1000 to buy stock in a firm or several firms in this industry. How much would you invest? Explain your decision based on the specific forces of competition affecting this industry.

This question is another approach to summing up the forces of competition affecting this industry. Students who spend a large percentage of the $1000 are gambling that firms will continue to achieve good profits and that stock prices rise. These students should discuss the lower influence that forces of competition, such as the threat of substitutes and the bargaining power of buyers, exert on the industry. These students may also perceive the medium level of rivalry among competitors sustaining profits in the near future.

Those who purchase small amounts should identify the forces of competition that will exert stronger influence on the industry and thereby affect company profits such as the power of stakeholders.

This short assessment technique will also reveal whether students understand the forces of competition and which ones, if any, may need further explanation.

Name:_____

ASSESSMENT FORM: STRATEGY SESSION 6

Directions: Answer the following problem on this sheet of paper.

You have a maximum of $1000 to buy stock in a firm or several firms in this industry. How much would you invest? Explain your decision based on the specific forces of competition affecting this industry.

_____

_____

_____

_____

_____

_____

_____

_____

_____

_____

_____

Generating a Plan of Action — SWOT Analysis

Exercise: An Action Plan for Robin Hood

OBJECTIVE

The SWOT model helps develop a comprehensive view of the firm in relation to its environment. By applying the SWOT approach to analysis, students can build a plan of action.

Time: 75 minutes

ADMINISTRATION

The exercise for this strategy session can be applied on an individual or group basis. For groups, ask students to first identify the S, W, O, and T individually. Then they can discuss the items, match the variables, and answer the questions in the Debriefing section that follows.

Note: to reduce in-class time, have students read the "Robin Hood" case before class.

Background

The SWOT approach, attributed to early business policy scholars such as Andrews, is a convenient method of classifying the internal aspects of a firm—its strengths and weaknesses—with the external environment in which it operates composed of opportunities and threats. This model supports a traditional notion in the field of strategy that there must be a good "fit" between the firm and its environment to ensure long-term performance. Although well known, it is also misused in the sense that the full benefit of the model is often not derived. It is most often used to produce a list of items describing the components without a clear direction as to what to do with this list. The introduction of the TOWS matrix solved that problem. This matrix made it clear that by matching the elements in the model, a set of action steps could be developed. When several consistent and viable steps are combined, they provide a plan of action that can be followed. For this reason, it provides the student with a method of moving beyond analysis to guidelines for action. As part of your instructions, it is important to reiterate to the students that:

1. They need to be as specific as possible while listing items. When the S, W, O, and T items are arrived at, they should be stated in a neutral form.
2. When items are matched, it must be stated in an actionable form.
3. At the stage of matching, they must try to identify as many as possible without trying to evaluate them.

DEBRIEFING

The exercise makes the student look at Robin Hood's operations as an organization. As part of the discussion, then, it will be useful for the instructor to constantly use business terminology to discuss the case.

Although this is a short case, it provides all the elements for applying a SWOT/TOWS, developing alternatives, and recommending a course of action.

Several common errors with the use of SWOT need to be stressed as part of the discussion:

- A common mistake students make is to confuse a weakness with a threat. The item in the students' matrix (Figure 7.1) includes the statement "Game (food) becoming scarce." Ask students why this would not be a "Weakness." Discuss that it belongs to the "Threats" category because it deals with a trend that is external to the firm.
- When an item is included, it should be spelled out so that it is clear why it is considered a strength or a threat. For example, if just the word "Size" were written in one of the boxes, it would be confusing, particularly since size can be both a "Strength" and "Weakness."
- Preferably, the comment should be as specific as possible.

Answers

Possible comments for SWOT analysis chart are shown in Figure 7.1 on page 52. Possible answers for Questions 1 and 2 in the student text follow:

1. The boxes SO, WO, ST and WT contain individual action steps. Some could be combined to generate two or more alternative courses of action. List the alternatives below.

   The action steps listed could be grouped into the following alternatives:

   1. **Expand operations by moving into other forests, raise more funds, and finance the release of King Richard while continuing to run the Merrymen.**
   2. **Stay with Sherwood Forest, introduce a transit tax selectively, and downsize operations by reducing size, and keeping some of the newcomers as a reserve force.**
   3. **Disband the Merrymen venture, join the barons, work to release King Richard and thereby turn legitimate.**
   4. **Kill the Sheriff.**

2. What criteria will you use to choose the action steps to follow?

   The basic purpose of the organization was to resist the unjust administration of the Sheriff, "Rob from the rich and give to the poor" is the present mission and would serve as a criteria. In addition, (a) risk of failure of the alternative; (b) personal values and character of Robin Hood—that is, top management team preferences; (c) short- vs. long-term horizon; and (d) resource constraints would serve as additional criteria for making a choice.

   Alternative 1 would fit the basic purpose, and it deals with growth without an undue risk of being personally involved in freeing Richard. Alternative 2 is conservative, and while

dealing with the problems, it does not take advantage of environmental opportunities. It is risk averse and does not fit with the character of the founder. Alternative 3 is a high-risk strategy and achieves the purpose of ultimately changing the administration. Alternative 4 is extreme; there is no evidence to suggest that the Sheriff's actions justify it, nor whether the act would be pardonable even if Richard were released.

General Comments

As part of the debriefing, the instructor can link the SWOT to the other models in strategic management by showing how the five-forces model of industry analysis can provide information to identify opportunities and favorable environmental trends as well as threats. The value chain concept can feed into strengths or weaknesses. In addition, thinking in terms of business functions (marketing, finance, administration, and so on) and management functions (planning, organizing, leading, and controlling) would serve as a checklist to arrive at strengths and weaknesses.

Ethics

An issue of ethics that can be raised in this case is whether the villagers should be accepting help from Robin Hood. Clearly, his activity is illegal, but knowing that he is offering stolen property, should the beneficiaries have any qualms?

ASSESSMENT

Collect the SWOT chart (Figure 7.1) from the students for grading purposes. Evaluate it based on:

1. Whether the S and W reflect only internal elements or threats have been included as part of weaknesses.
2. Whether the items have been stated in a neutral form.
3. Whether the elements that have been matched reveal an action step or just describe a consequence. Since few students think of how the mission of the group would serve as a basis to evaluate the alternatives, the instructor can give extra points to those who do.

REFERENCES

Andrews, K. R. 1980. *The Concept of Corporate Strategy*. Homewood, IL: Richard D. Irwin

Hill, T. and R. Westbrook. 1997. SWOT analysis: It's time for a product recall. *Long Range Planning* 30(1): 46–52.

Weihrich, H. 1982. The TOWS Matrix-A tool for situational analysis. *Long Range Planning* 15(2): 54–66.

Figure 7.1   Answers for SWOT Analysis Chart for "Robin Hood"

INTERNAL

	Strengths	Weaknesses
	1. Size: more fighting men 2. Robin's leadership—ideals 3. Established brand—fear of the Merrymen 4. Delegation of tasks to lieutenants (hierarchical positions)	1. Size: becoming unmanageable 2. Centralized decision making by Robin 3. Discipline among followers, new recruits not sharing founder's ideals 4. Finances: revenues falling, and costs of feeding etc., increasing
Opportunities (Favorable Trends) 1. Transit tax 2. Other forests available 3. Barons are looking for allies 4. Political amnesty is available 5. People will be willing to support organizations that oppose the king (will pay taxes)	**SO** 1. Expand operations to other forests (S1, O1) 2. Form political party through alliances with barons to release King (S1,S3, O2, O3)	**WO** 1. Join barons and disband Merrymen (W1, W3, O3) 2. Levy transit tax (W4, O4)
Threats (Unfavorable Trends) 1. Game (food) becoming scarce 2. Travelers finding alternative routes 3. Sheriff getting organized and stronger 4. Sheriff's men infiltrate Merrymen	**ST** 1. Kill the Sheriff (S1, T3) 2. Create separate group with a different mission—to hunt for food and not involved in robbing (S1, T1)	**WT** 1. Reduce operations to a manageable size (W1, W3, T1) 2. Create two divisions—one for current operations and another as reserve force (W1, W4, T1) 3. Limit who can join Merrymen (by changing identity of Robin Hood's group (W1, W3, T4)

EXTERNAL

Exercise: Choosing How to Compete in the Lodging Industry

OBJECTIVE

In this session's exercise, students compare organizations pursuing each of the four generic strategies—and they compare a firm that is stuck in the middle.

Time: 90 minutes

ADMINISTRATION

Materials

Bring enough posters (one per group) —such as the Post-It Easel Pad by 3M Co.—and markers for each group.

Process

Step 1

Depending on your class's size, have students form into groups of four to six. Each group is assigned a generic strategy (Company A = cost leadership; Company B = differentiator; Company C = focus cost leadership; Company D = focus differentiator). One group, which will be Company E, is assigned the stuck-in-the-middle strategy. If there are more than 30 students, then more than one group may be assigned to the same strategy. As an alternative, the instructor can write the strategy on pieces of paper and ask a representative from each team to come forward and pick one. (Students should not reveal what their assigned "strategy" is.)

Step 2

Tell the groups that they are the top management teams of a new hotel company entering the lodging industry and to follow the guidelines in the exercise as they prepare a poster depicting their hotel and presentation. (It helps to ask the students to draft the poster on a sheet of paper before attempting to put the information down on the poster.) Encourage students to incorporate drawings and to be creative in terms of hotel design, room layout, advertising slogans, and so on. The poster is used to sell the idea of the hotel and the organization to potential investors who might want to fund the company as it attempts to capture its target market. Instruct students to compare the information on the generic strategy charts they prepared on an individual basis (see "Debriefing" below) in order to generate ideas for the poster and presentation. The group that is assigned the "stuck-in-the-middle" strategy (Company E) should be encouraged to

choose elements from the cost leadership and differentiation strategies. Advise the group that the purpose of including this strategy option in the exercise is to show the class why the cost leadership and differentiation strategies cannot be used together to develop an overall posture toward the market.
(45 minutes)

Step 3

After the assigned time has elapsed, have each group post its board on the wall. Instruct all students to take a tour examining the various hotels that have been created. (5 minutes)

Step 4

Call on each group to present their proposed lodging property and their organization as they would to potential investors. For the presentation, instruct groups to focus on discussing guideline items dealing with skills and resources, features of the organization, and environmental trends. Instruct teams not to reveal their intended strategy during the presentation. At the end of each presentation, ask the class to identify the strategy. (40 minutes).

Winning Strategy Option

Another technique is to give each person in class one small post-it note with instructions that this is their $100,000 to invest. They are welcome to walk around the class and invest it by sticking it on the poster that they think has the most clear, winning strategy. They are, however, not to invest in their own company. After the students have done their rounds, the poster with the maximum stickers on it is the winner.

DEBRIEFING

To promote individual accountability, particularly if the group exercise is done in class, we ask students to prepare the chart titled "Identifying the Characteristics of the Four Kinds of Generic Strategies" in the exercise on an individual basis as a homework assignment. The charts are collected at the start of class and either returned to the students after a quick scan, or they are kept for grading purposes. A sample solution is shown in Table 8.1.

Students quickly realize that before constructing a hotel, they must identify and articulate the various parameters of the organization and its environment, including the profile of the buyer/customer group and its potential for growth in the future.

If more than one group presents a poster board on the same strategy, their approaches are inevitably different. This highlights the impact of individual talent and organizational culture on the implementation of a generic strategy. It can also lead to an interesting debate in class as to whether a particular feature described by one group really supports their generic strategy.

Students are encouraged to draw pictures and use their creativity in the development of their poster board. Their only instructions are that it should be interesting and convey the general essence of their hotel property and their organization. The freedom to operate outside the bounds of reality in creating the poster introduces humor and levity to the discussions.

To stress the organizational impact of the strategy, remind students that their presentation is not for marketing purposes. In addition to positioning, ad slogans, and so on, their target audience of investors will be looking for information about how the organization possesses the skills to support the strategy they are following.

The exercise forces students to discuss competitive positioning and issues of aligning the various organizational elements with the generic strategy. Table 8.2 shows some examples.

Table 8.1   Identifying the Characteristics of the Four Kinds of Generic Strategies

Strategy	Company Features and Description	Target Market	Environmental Trends That Support Strategy	Environmental Trends That Threaten Strategy
Cost leadership: Company A (Similar to Best Western, Super 8, etc.)	No frills in the hotel in order to keep costs low. Modest entryway (no fancy lobby). Guest rooms are comfortable and sizable but without extra amenities. Basic services include TV and phone. No restaurant in the hotel but located near a chain (e.g., Denny's). No room service or dry cleaning available. Company keeps costs lower in order to offer economical room rates.	Mass market—any market segment that values low-price lodging (families, business or vacation travelers)	High gas prices and airline rates result in some travelers looking to save money on room rental. Lifestyle trends: multiple vacations during the year are common; vacation budgets can be stretched further with low-priced accommodations	Continuing strong economy makes demand for this alternative weaker than when economic conditions are poor. Overbuilding in this segment during the 1990s resulted in an over-abundance of rooms (supply).
Differentiator: Company B (Similar to Hilton or Hyatt)	These properties cater to consumers who want luxury and convenience. Rooms include amenities such as irons, hair dryers, shampoo and other toiletries. TV with cable and HBO included. Restaurants, entertainment/lounges saunas, pools, massage facilities, hair salons, clothing stores, etc., are also included on the premises. Optional services (dry cleaning and room service) are available. Rooms and furnishings are plush. Company must charge higher rates for extra accommodations and services.	Mass market—any market segment that values service and luxury (families, business or vacation travelers). These consumers will pay more for extra accommodations and services.	Continuing strong economy results in more discretionary income for consumers.	Strong economy has resulted in low unemployment thus aggravating the shortage of workers for service industries.
Focus cost leadership: Company C* (Similar to LaQuinta, which targets only business and professional travelers.)	No frills to keep costs low. Modest entryway (no fancy lobby). Guest rooms comfortable and sizable but without extra amenities. Basic services include TV and phone. No restaurant—but located near a chain (Denny's). No room service available. Company keeps costs lower in order to offer economical room rates.	Business travelers who are compensated on a per diem rate.	High gas prices and airline rates can be offset by room rentals. This is particularly important when business people have limited daily expenses that are covered.	Businesses are prospering and reducing expense accounts is less of a priority during boom periods. Overbuilding of this segment (economy properties) during the 1990s continues to result in a glut in room supply.

Table 8.1   Identifying the Characteristics of the Four Kinds of Generic Strategies (cont.)

Strategy	Company Features and Description	Target Market	Environmental Trends That Support Strategy	Environmental Trends That Threaten Strategy
Focus differentiator: Company D* (Similar to XV Beacon in Boston; New York, New York; & Oceanas Apart with rates starting at $395/night.)	Deluxe room accommodations. Pool, sauna, full restaurant and lounge on the property. Voicemail, fax, and copy services. Small conference rooms on each floor. Complementary breakfast. Company must charge higher rates for extra accommodations and services.	Business executives who will pay more for extra accommodations and services.	Continuing strong economy and strong business climate reduces likelihood of expense reductions.	Strong economy has resulted in low unemployment. This is aggravating the shortage of workers for service industries.
Stuck in the middle: Company E	Rooms furnished with few amenities. Décor is plain. TV with HBO available for a fee. Room service offered during limited hours. Small coffee shop-type restaurant on the premise open from 8:00 a.m. to 7:00 p.m., Monday through Saturday. Outdoor pool. Room rentals are higher than economy properties due to the extra costs associated with staffing the restaurant, maintaining the pool, and providing room service.	Travelers without children in the 20 to 30 age group and adults 50 and older.	Continuing strong economy provides more discretionary income for travelers who want some services but do not want to pay high room rates.	Targeting adults 50 and older takes advantage of a demographic trend (large portions of the "baby boom" population has reached this age).
*Focus strategies are segmentation strategies, which are increasingly being used by this industry to spur growth.				

Table 8.2   Alignment of Various Organizational Elements with the Generic Strategy

Generic Strategy	Skills and Resources	Organizational Requirements (Structure, Incentive Systems, etc.)
Cost Leadership	▪ Intense supervision of labor ▪ Attention to process or operational details ▪ Emphasis on cost cutting measures ▪ Low cost supplier arrangements	▪ Frequent and detailed control reports ▪ Structured organization and responsibilities ▪ Incentives based on meeting strict quantitative targets
Differentiation	▪ Strong marketing skills ▪ Creative flair ▪ Reputation for quality leadership ▪ Superior customer responsiveness	▪ Strong coordination among functions in marketing, customer service, and operations ▪ Incentives that reward employees for satisfying customers beyond normal levels (subjective measurement and incentives instead of quantitative measures) ▪ Amenities to attract highly skilled labor

Table 8.2   Alignment of Various Organizational Elements with the Generic Strategy (cont.)

Generic Strategy	Skills and Resources	Organizational Requirements (Structure, Incentive Systems, etc.)
Focus	• Cost leadership skills and resources directed at a particular buyer group/ market segment; or • Differentiator skills and resources directed at a particular buyer group/market segment	• Cost leadership organizational requirements directed at a particular buyer group/market segment; or • Differentiator organizational requirements directed at a particular buyer group/market segment

ASSESSMENT: WHAT IS THE POINT?

If time is available at the end of class or at the beginning of the next class, hand out index cards and ask students to identify three or four important points that the exercise demonstrated. Put the following statement on the board and ask students to fill in the bullets:

The poster and presentation exercise illustrated the following four points:

1. _____

2. _____

3. _____

4. _____

This assessment is designed to add a reflection component to the exercise. This is an important aspect, particularly since the humorous poster designs may sidetrack some of the students. In addition to refocusing student attention on the generic strategy topic, the assessment will also demonstrate faculty respect for and interest in student feedback. Let the class know in advance that you will respond at the start of the next class to the feedback by identifying the most commonly raised learning points. This also provides a unique twist on the typical instructor summary of material to one that is based on student feedback.

Strategy Session 9

Viewing Corporate Strategy from the Core Competencies Perspective

Exercise: Corporate Strategy at Walt Disney Company

OBJECTIVE

This session's exercise gives students practice in designing corporate strategy for a diversified company from a core competencies perspective.

Time: 75 minutes

ADMINISTRATION

Depending on time constraints, the instructor can perform Strategy Session 9 three ways. The first option is to have students do the reading before class and work on the exercise individually in class and then in teams. The second option is to do the reading *and* the exercise in class. The third option is to have students complete both the reading and exercise before class. This option frees up time for group work and end-of-the-class discussion.

When assigning the reading and exercise before class, give students the preassessment form at the start of class. Allocate a small portion of the grade for these assignments. In addition, allow five minutes for the short-answer assessment form to be completed.

Place students in teams of three or five. Each team completes the in-class worksheet that guides them through the inventory of Disney core competencies and product-markets in two time frames. Students then evaluate the company's current situation in terms of the inventory. Allow 20 minutes for this group assignment.

Reconvene the class. Have one or two of the groups present their analysis. Discuss future corporate strategy based on these analyses.

Preassessment

The optional preassessment form—reproduced at the end of these instructor notes for this session—can be given to students on an individual basis before class. Allocate a portion of the grade for these quiz-type assessments. The goal is to gauge the level of student understanding of the material before the in-class exercise. Students pay closer attention to the concepts from the reading and case information when they know they will be assessed on an individual basis.

Preassessment Answers

1. When the Walt Disney Company started and through the early 1980s, what was its core competence or competencies? Briefly discuss.

Disney's initial core skill was in **creative animation.** What distinguished the company in its early days was Walt Disney's **attention to detail** and his search for **innovative production techniques** to bring characters to life. These core skills combined to help create the company's competence in developing **creative entertainment experiences,** especially for families.

2. What product lines were linked to the company's core competencies during this period (up to the early 1980s)?

    Short animation clips were the first product linkage to the core competence of creative animation. These clips gave the newly formed partnership between Walt Disney and his brother Roy practice in creating characters that were realistic. For example, the first animated movie—*Steamboat Willie*—used sound to make the animated characters more lifelike.

    This company's skill in creative animation resulted **in full-length feature films that introduced a stable of famous cartoon characters.** Using the expertise developed in filmmaking, the company then created live-action films about **fantasy characters,** such as Davy Crockett and Mary Poppins to name a few. The skill of creative animation had been leveraged to creative filmmaking for family entertainment. By 1960, the company was unique in its ability to combine animation and live-action films.

    The company's skill in developing creative entertainment experiences was then leveraged to start **Disney theme parks.** As a result, families experienced first-hand the fun and fantasy that had become Disney's mission. **The Disney Channel** came on line in 1983, and **licensing** of the famous Disney characters was another product-market area that developed during the early years.

3. What other product lines and markets have been developed to date?

    As part of Michael Eisner's growth strategy, the company expanded its products and markets: more theme parks, Disney Stores, cruise ships, hotels, television and cable station ownership, radio stations, a broadcast network, Web sites. In addition, production of animated and live-action films continued. Some of these ventures had a direct relationship to Disney's unique ability to provide creative entertainment experiences. The company's Go.com subsidiary, which is a search engine similar to Yahoo, has no direct linkage to the company's core competencies developed to date.

4. Have any new core competencies been developed? Briefly discuss.

    Although the Disney Company has evolved into an entertainment empire, the primary change in competencies has been the enhancement of the company's technology skills, particularly in terms of theme park attractions and move production. However, due to the company's aggressive growth, the number of holdings made it more difficult for management to pay close attention to detail, one of the original core competencies of this organization. Eisner's appointment of Robert Iger as president and chief operating officer is expected to result in Eisner spending more time in day-to-day operations, particularly in movie production, theme park rides, and Disney Store redesign.

Team Activity

The purpose of the in-class team activity is to give students an opportunity to develop an inventory of Disney core competencies and product-markets similar to the way it occurs in organizations. That is, a team of senior managers—versus one or two managers individually—participate in the process of identifying core competencies. As Hamel and Prahalad advise, a firm cannot actively manage core competencies if managers do not share a view of what those core competencies are. This team activity simulates the type of meetings and discussions that would occur in generating that shared understanding.

The form "Disney Core Competencies Portfolio"—reproduced at the end of these instructor notes for this session—is similar to the one in the students' text that they prepared on an individual basis as part of the exercise. However, in teams they are asked to generate a newly agreed-upon listing and to identify areas where linkages appear to be lacking.

Class Discussion

Scale for Linking Competencies to New Product-Markets as of 2000

Start the session by comparing team ratings and recording each team's score on the board. The rating provides a comparative summary of each team's conclusion regarding the core competencies portfolio of Walt Disney Company as of the end of the case. There is no "correct" score, and arguments can be made for any of the ratings. However, the company's recent efforts to sell off noncore operations suggest that the linkage was not as strong between core competencies and product-markets during the Eisner acquisition period as it was before that time.

Core Competencies and Product-Markets

The next phase of the class discussion is comparing the core competencies and product-markets chart (see Figure 9.1).

Then discuss the specifics in the chart that led to the team ratings. Typically, students easily note the linkage between core competencies and product lines in the early time frame of 1923–1983. However, in the later time frame, the goal of building an entertainment empire and, in particular, the acquisition of Capital Cities/ABC, Inc. expanded Disney's holdings to noncore operations. The company has added new product-markets but many are not leveraging existing core competencies.

In fact, students notice that the company's core competencies were not the driving force behind the aggressive growth strategy. This is evident in the company's efforts to pare down noncore operations, which began in late 1999 and continue today. Specifically, Disney sold its Fairchild Publications unit and is considering the sale of *Los Angeles* magazine; and although it had not found a buyer for its baseball and hockey teams, Disney has explored the sale of these entities as well.

Another issue is that coordination of a large multidivisional organization becomes more complex as new product lines and markets are added, and Disney top management may have been spread too thinly to adequately control a growing empire. In late 1999, it shut down its burgeoning chain of Club Disney entertainment centers and combined some television production operations. In fact, issues of control were identified when Robert Iger was appointed as Disney's president and chief operating officer in January 2000. Eisner announced both he and Iger would be handling increased detail work and in particular cost-cutting initiatives.

Some students may also note that the creative animation competence of past years has shifted its focus towards the technology used in movies and away from the plot line and character development. For example, although the movie *Dinosaurs* did well in initial ticket sales, its high production costs and the less-than-enthusiastic reviews about its story and characters made it vulnerable to strong competitors, such as DreamWorks SKG.

Figure 9.1   Core Competencies and Product-Markets

	Core Competencies	Product-markets	Areas where linkages between core competencies and product-markets are lacking
1923–1983	• Creative animation • Attention to detail • Innovative production techniques • Creative entertainment experiences	• Short animation clips • Full-length feature films that introduced famous cartoon characters • Fantasy character development • Disney theme parks • Disney channel • Licensing of famous characters	The company's core competencies were leveraged across all product-markets. Further synergy was created since the combination of theme parks, television, and movies fed on and promoted each other.
1984–2000	The listing of core competencies is similar to those above. However, due to the size of the company, attention to detail no longer was distinctive, and the company may be moving away from an emphasis on plot line and character development towards a focus on technology innovation.	• Animated films and TV episodes • Live-action films and TV episodes • Theme parks • Hotels • Cruise ships • Disney Stores • Broadcast network (ABC) • TV stations • International Disney channels • Radio stations • Internet portal (Go.com) • 5 web sites • Interests in 9 cable networks • Magazine publications	The company's core competencies were not the driving force behind the aggressive growth strategy that occurred during 1995. A focus on core competencies was replaced with the desire to build an entertainment empire.

Discussion Question

Discuss the question (item 3) of whether the company should develop new core competencies, leverage existing skills into new business areas, or continue to sell off units? Consider the following:

- Is Disney still relying on the old "standby" characters (Goofy, Mickey Mouse, Donald Duck) that resulted from Walt Disney's creative talents? Are the new characters (the Little Mermaid, Mulan, Hercules) developed during Eisner's era as marketable? Should the company consider "buying" new characters, such as Pokémon?
- Is the management of Disney Company becoming more focused on the organizational and administrative operation of running a large entertainment empire rather than on sustaining its creative expertise?

BCG Comparison

Instructors can compare the portfolio of core competencies to the Boston Consulting Group (BCG) portfolio framework to examine the strategies each might suggest. In the BCG matrix shown below, the consumer products division ends up in the low or "dog" category because of the low growth associated with the retail industry and the company's low market share in relation to other retailers. Its strategy should be to sell off the division. The theme parks division is considered the company's "cash cow," as described in a *Business Week* article, and would be the funding source for moving other divisions into the "star" category (top left box):

	High	Studio entertainment	Media networks Go.com
Industry Growth			
	Low	Theme parks	Consumer products
		High	Low

Relative Market Share

ASSESSMENT

At the end of the session or at the start of the next class, ask students to complete an "Application Card." This technique tells whether the students understand the theory of core competence and gets them thinking about the potential uses of what they are learning.

Hand out an index card and write the following instructions on the board:

1. Briefly, discuss how the concept of a portfolio of core competence can be applied to organizations that operate in one industry.
2. What is this college's/university's core competence?

Alternatively, if the class has recently discussed a case concerning a multidivisional firm, change the instructions on the board to:

> Having read and discussed the portfolio of core competence model, summarize the core competence or competencies of XYZ company.

Three to five minutes is usually enough time for the students to complete the application card. Collect the cards and let students know when they will get feedback. The instructor can determine quickly whether the application is accurate, especially if students identify a unique value-creating capability or core skill of their college or university. Share with the class four or five of the best examples.

Students who come up with poor or incorrect examples are likely to remember and learn the bad examples. Be sure to allocate time for follow-up. Also, encourage students to keep an "applications journal" in their class notebooks. This learning process can also be reinforced if questions like the ones written on the board for this assessment are included as part of an exam or written assignment that students are told will be graded.

Name: _____

PREASSESSMENT FORM: STRATEGY SESSION 9

Directions: Answer the following questions on this sheet of paper.

1. When the Walt Disney Company started and through the early 1980s, what was its core competence or competencies? Briefly discuss.

    _____

    _____

    _____

    _____

    _____

    _____

2. What product lines were linked to the company's core competencies during this period (up to the early 1980s)?

    _____

    _____

    _____

    _____

    _____

    _____

3. Have any new core competencies been developed? Briefly discuss.

_____

_____

_____

_____

_____

_____

_____

4. Have any new core competencies been developed? Briefly discuss.

_____

_____

_____

_____

_____

_____

_____

Names: _____

_____

1. Complete the information as a team for Disney Company in the boxes below. Identify areas where linkages between core competencies and product-markets are not as apparent.

	Core Competencies	Product-markets	Areas where linkages between core competencies and product-markets are lacking
1923–1983			
1984–2000			

2. What is the team's opinion of how well the company, as it exists in 2000, has linked its core competencies to new product-markets:

Rating = _____

5 = Linkage is the strongest that it has been in the company's history.

4 = Linkage is improving as a result of new product-markets (during the Eisner era).

3 = Linkage is the same before and during the Eisner era.

2 = Link is getting weaker as a result of new product-markets (during the Eisner era).

1 = No linkage between core competencies and product-markets exists.

3. Briefly, discuss whether you think the company should develop new core competencies, leverage existing skills into new business areas, or continue to sell off units?

_____

_____

_____

_____

_____

_____

_____

_____

_____

Exercise: Making the General Motors-Toyota Alliance Work

OBJECTIVE

This session's exercise helps students understand the motivations that drive companies to form strategic alliances—and the importance of the managerial effort required in making them work.

Time: 75 minutes

ADMINISTRATION

Before Class

Instruct the students to complete the reading, case, and Question 1 of the exercise.

In Class

Form groups of three students, with one student each representing Toyota and GM, and one serving as an observer. If you wish to have fewer groups, you could have teams of five with two students each representing Toyota and GM, and one as the observer.

Announce to the students that the existing alliance contract between GM and Toyota has come up for renewal. The task for each team is to negotiate a revision to the agreement. After completion of negotiation, the students answer the remaining questions in the exercise. The role of the observer is to make notes on the progress of the negotiation. An observer's form, attached, may be used for this purpose. The instructor may allow the observers to interrupt and help the process along if they find the parties are stuck on some issues.

Before start of the negotiation:

1. Give the representatives of GM and Toyota in each team a copy of the additional information given at the end of this session's notes. Inform them that the other party does not have the same information.
2. Give a copy of the Observer's Report, also provided at the end of this session's notes, to the observer in each team, which is to be completed after the negotiation has taken place.

Allow five minutes for the company representatives to develop objectives and formulate a negotiation strategy. Allow 25 minutes for negotiation, ten minutes for completion of forms, and 25 minutes for debriefing.

DEBRIEFING

Question 1

What are the areas of cooperation and conflict that arise from the NUMMI alliance? Try to separate the issues you would consider strategic and operational for the organization.

Table 10.1 shows a typical answer.

Table 10.1 Areas of Cooperation and Conflict

	Cooperation	Conflict
Strategic	<ul><li>Globalizing the corporate strategy (GM and Toyota)</li><li>Fill in gaps in GM product line</li><li>Strengthen U.S. presence (Toyota)</li></ul>	<ul><li>R & D in small car design since Toyota may not want to give up its skills here</li></ul>
Operational	<ul><li>Production of models agreed upon.</li><li>Incorporating new work methods (GM learn about Toyota's famous production system)</li><li>Learn how to work with UAW and U.S. suppliers (Toyota)</li></ul>	<ul><li>Deals with union that may not be acceptable at other GM plants</li><li>Philosophy regarding worker empowerment varies between U.S. and Japanese management</li></ul>

Combining the high and low possibilities of conflict and cooperation, Yoshino and Rangan identify four types of alliances. This framework is useful in discussing this exercise because it establishes the reasons for the role of alliances in both competitive and noncompetitive situations.

- A **procompetitive** alliance usually takes place between players in two different industries, where they are part of a vertical value chain, such as suppliers and distributors. Conflict is low since they are not rivals. The firms can work closely to develop processes and generate savings for mutual benefit. Japanese firms are known for developing long-term relations with their suppliers that would fall in this category. Interaction between the firms will be relatively low.
- **Noncompetitive** alliances are within the industry but among firms that do not compete because they fall in different strategic groups. For instance, firms may seek an alliance with another to develop technologies useful for both or to complement their product lines. GM's alliance with Isuzu—to jointly develop a small car—is an example.
- **Competitive** alliances, such as the one between GM and Toyota in the NUMMI venture, have the highest potential for interaction and rivalry. However, partners need to be careful about leakage of information, and protect their competencies. Learning possibilities are high.

- **Precompetitive** alliances are often between firms from different industries to work on clearly defined activities such as technology development. Interaction is limited to researchers.

Questions 2–4

These questions are meant to probe the various routes the negotiations could take. Information provided to the students separately on Toyota and GM generates a wide range in the negotiations. They include:

1. Continuing NUMMI without any change;
2. Continuing NUMMI with increased safeguards for both parties against raiding personnel, and so on;
3. Restructuring the agreement with GM having a minority holding; and
4. Dissolving the agreement with Toyota buying out GM.

Instructors should probe the reasons for each team's conclusions. While discussing responses to these questions, instructors should ask the observers to report from their notes on the level of trust that was displayed, and whether the two parties shared information that was given to them as confidential, and the like. Instructors can introduce a variation by telling some teams that the information is confidential and not priming other teams on this.

In the case of long-term collaborations, trust plays an important part if the relationship is to be successful. However, to remember former President Reagan's famous dictum in relations with the erstwhile Soviet Union, the principle must be "Trust but verify." The firm must clearly identify what it intends to learn from the partner, break it down into identifiable elements and measure those elements. Progress must be monitored continuously and when it is perceived that the alliance is falling short of expectations, a meeting with the partner may be necessary to revisit the agreement and make changes.

Question 5

"How would you judge whether NUMMI is a success or not?" Some students may point out that it would be difficult to judge NUMMI due to the lack of financial data. In terms of labor-management relations, absenteeism, and the like, the case suggests that improvement occurred in these areas. Another indication of success is the continuing existence of NUMMI, although termination of an alliance does not necessarily mean failure. It can signal that objectives have been accomplished.

However, two other issues need to be considered. One is that NUMMI was formed to satisfy the objectives of its two parents. Apart from the financial performance of NUMMI, one should be able to see if the partners are achieving their objectives. Even if an alliance was not performing well by normal accounting measures, it could be meeting partners' objectives and thus be considered successful.

A second issue is that collaboration between GM and Toyota has extended to several other areas such as research and marketing arrangements in Japan. In evaluating GM's alliance with Toyota, it may be too restrictive to examine only the NUMMI venture and exclude the other benefits that the two have derived.

Several GM executives have spent time at NUMMI and brought back information about teamwork, JIT, and so on, and these measures have been implemented at other GM plants. As the case shows, though the Corolla and Geo Prizm are identical, customer perceptions vary and that has to do with the respective images of the partners in the marketplace.

Although GM has learned from NUMMI, the charge that this "education" is superficial needs to be taken seriously. They did not consciously manage the evolution of a new strategy based on what was learned from the alliance. It is believed that in the absence of a clearly enunciated policy, middle management was not aware of how to make use of the alliance experience. While teamwork, just-in-time, and other worker and production techniques have been introduced in GM plants, the underlying philosophy of managing the enterprise—or even the production function—remains the same. More recently, even though the Saturn venture of GM was initiated as a very different enterprise, efforts are in progress to bring Saturn within the total gambit of GM. If GM is moving back to "consolidating" its activities to a familiar model, it may be less inclined to learn from alliances in the future.

Finally, in addition to the stated goals of the alliance, another measure of the success would be to examine the extent to which the venture has met the separate goals of the two partners. Not knowing what these are—the information is not being in the public domain—discussion can only be speculative.

ASSESSMENT

Use the form at the end of this session's instructor's notes for assessment It can be administered at the beginning of the next class. Suggested answers for the assessment questions follow:

1. How was NUMMI structured to enable the companies to benefit from the alliance?

    Answer:

    a. Sharing of Board representation equally.
    b. GM: Liaison center to co-ordinate learning from alliance; rotation of executives.

       By making it a 50:50 venture, both firms signaled an equal commitment to the experience.

       Toyota, given its background of being a part of a *keiretsu*, is more attuned to working cooperatively with different organizations.

2. Would an alliance between Microsoft and Intel be considered procompetitive—that is, players in two different industries—or noncompetitive—that is, same industry but firms that do not compete?

    Answer: If the computer industry is defined broadly, the alliance could be considered noncompetitive. If hardware and software were considered separate industries, the alliance would be considered procompetitive. Using the Value Net model based on game theory, the two firms are complementors. An alliance between them helps establish standards, but can also be accused of closing out innovation.

3. Should alliances between competitors be regulated?

    Answer: This is meant to stimulate responses in terms of the role of alliances within the competitive and antitrust policy of the nation. Some students would argue in favor of regulation since alliances could be a disguise for cooperation on pricing, or carving up a market, and these would be antitrust issues. Others would say that the market should be allowed to determine whether the alliance works or not, and there is no need for government intervention.

REFERENCES

DeBare, Ilana. 1998. NUMMI faces blow if GM cuts Prizm. *The San Francisco Chronicle*, September 24: B1

Harvard Business School. 1988. *General Motors' Asian Alliances*, Case #9-388-094

Shirouzu, Norihiko. 2000. Toyota, GM mull plant for hybrids. *Wall Street Journal*, April 6: A3.

Name: _____

ASSESSMENT FORM: STRATEGY SESSION 10

1. How was NUMMI structured to enable the companies to benefit from the alliance?

_____

_____

_____

_____

_____

_____

_____

2. Would an alliance between Microsoft and Intel be considered procompetitive (i.e., players in two different industries) or noncompetitive (i.e., same industry but firms that do not compete)?

_____

_____

_____

_____

_____

_____

_____

_____

_____

_____

_____

_____

3. Should alliances between competitors be regulated?

_____

_____

_____

_____

_____

Handout for Strategy Session 10

FOR GM STUDENTS

GM and Toyota have made progress in developing an electric-gasoline hybrid vehicle as part of a five-year joint research project in alternative-propulsion technology. They might consider manufacturing the hybrid at NUMMI. No definite conclusions have been reached although "several scenarios" are being considered.

The NUMMI plant produces GM's entire Prizm line, whose sales have been falling since 1994. The company might drop the Prizm, which competes against other small GM sedans like the Chevy Cavalier, Pontiac Sunfire, and some Saturn models. A definite decision had not been taken on the issue.

GM is aware Toyota has plans to expand manufacturing in North America and is currently expanding its Canadian plant.

GM's production system currently allows it to assemble a car within 17 to 18 days of an order. It would like to shorten this to the extent possible and stay competitive. It is aware that Toyota has designed a new production system that allows it to produce a car within 5 days of an order and is likely to implement it in NUMMI.

FOR TOYOTA STUDENTS

GM and Toyota have made progress in developing an electric-gasoline hybrid vehicle as part of a five-year joint research project in alternative-propulsion technology. Toyota's Prius, its hybrid in Japan, gets 66 miles per gallon of gasoline and it sees a big market for the product in the United States, where it is scheduled to launch soon.

GM and Toyota might consider manufacturing the hybrid at NUMMI. However, Toyota has a commitment not to have layoffs in the plant and feels increasing capacity may jeopardize the labor management stability there. A Toyota executive, who did not want to be quoted, said he would "prefer" to build a new plant from scratch. Toyota is also considering whether it should buyout GM's share of the NUMMI plant.

Toyota recently announced that it has found a way to produce a car within five days of a customer order. This is based on sophisticated computer software that allows planners to create a simulated production line 15 days ahead, which is constantly revised, and generates orders to suppliers for parts. Toyota intends to apply this system in the NUMMI plant after trials in its Ontario plant.

Observer's Report: GM-Toyota Alliance*

Name:_____

Names of Negotiators:

Toyota: _____

GM: _____

    Your role is to observe the negotiation process between the two players. Your notes can cover the following issues:

1. Toyota's objective in the negotiation appeared to be:

_____

_____

_____

_____

2. GM's objective in the negotiation appeared to be:

_____

_____

_____

_____

---

* Form adapted from John K. Butler. 1996. After Nafta: A cross-cultural negotiation exercise. *Simulation and Games* 27(4): 507–516

For the statements below, please circle the appropriate answer:

		Strongly Disagree		Neutral		Strongly Agree
3.	Toyota tried hard to get what it needed.	1	2	3	4	5
4.	Toyota shared *relevant* information with GM.	1	2	3	4	5
5.	GM tried hard to get what it needed.	1	2	3	4	5
6.	GM shared *relevant* information with Toyota.	1	2	3	4	5
7.	GM seemed to trust Toyota.	1	2	3	4	5
8.	Toyota seemed to trust GM.	1	2	3	4	5
9.	The final agreement appeared to satisfy both parties.	1	2	3	4	5
10.	The two parties went into sufficient detail in the agreement.	1	2	3	4	5
11.	The two parties discussed mechanisms to monitor progress on the agreement.	Yes				No
12.	The two parties signed a contract.	Yes				No

13. Please describe briefly the process that the two parties used to negotiate.

_____

_____

_____

_____

_____

_____

_____

_____

Exercise: Global Operations of Bata Shoe and Nike

OBJECTIVE

This strategy session lets students understand two generic transnational strategies, namely global and multidomestic, commonly mentioned in strategic management literature to describe companies that operate globally.

Time: 45 minutes

ADMINISTRATION

This is a shorter exercise that can be administered in class during a 45-minute segment. There is no need for students to do prior preparation. The reading gives the students a brief description of the two strategies and then presents them with short profiles of two companies: Bata and Nike. Both companies are major global players in the footwear industry. Nike focuses on the athletic footwear market, with an image of high performance footwear endorsed by successful celebrity athletes. Bata focuses on mass-merchandized footwear for a broad cross-section of consumers, stressing value for money.

Performed individually, this exercise allows students about 15 minutes to complete the reading and about ten minutes to respond to the questions. The remaining 20 minutes can be used for debriefing.

DEBRIEFING

Review the questions for discussion. Through a show of hands, tally the most frequent student response to the question. Maintain a score on the board with three columns: one for the question number, one each for Bata and Nike. Within the company columns, put the number that has the largest show of hands.

The main variables that classify multinational organizations are:

- Environment/industry
- Corporate level strategy
- Organizational design
- Subsidiary strategy/role
- Subsidiary structure
- Control mechanisms
- Human resource practices

Answers to Questions

The questions in the exercise are designed to cover these variables. They illustrate how the different strategies followed by the companies are reflected in their strategic and operational decisions. Finally, the students are asked to identify the applicable transnational strategy in Question 9 after identifying operational details in the earlier questions.

1. The company perceives its target consumers as having similar needs across the globe.

2. The firm's definition of the industry encompasses several segments.

    The first question is intended to generate discussion. Both companies perceive their target consumers as having similar needs across the globe. (For this reason, both are closer to 5 on the scale for question 1. They differ in the market segment that they target. Nike believes that athletes and sports enthusiasts have similar needs and expectations from their footwear anywhere in the globe. Similarly, Bata is providing low to medium priced footwear for the common person across the globe.

    Of the two, Bata takes a broader view of the industry and is more likely to offer a range of footwear to serve different needs and respond more to local markets.

3. The parent company is considering diversifying into sporting apparel (swimwear) or fitness equipment. It believes it already has some competence within the company and familiarity with markets to be able to venture into it. This diversification fits with the present strategy followed by the company.

    Bata would probably be rated a 1 or 2 on the scale; Nike would be a 4 or 5. This statement deals with a corporate level diversification decision. This largely fits with the style of Nike rather than Bata. The nature of the product, sporting apparel or fitness equipment, would appeal to their current customers, and the company understands the needs of these consumers. Moreover, it is in the nature of Nike to make a diversification decision like this. Bata runs semi-autonomous companies targeted at the low to medium end of the scale and is not really focused on athletics and fitness. The experience of Bata India shows that it has limited skills in moving away from its target markets.

4. If a marketing manager wished to launch a new promotional campaign, he or she would need to obtain prior approval from the parent company.

    Bata—1 or 2; Nike—4 or 5. Marketing is a centrally controlled activity in Nike, and therefore there is less likely to be a country manager. If there were one, the Nike manager would more likely need parent company approval than the Bata manager.

5. If a production manager wished to change hiring or training practices, he or she would need to obtain prior approval from the parent company.

    Bata—1 or 2; Nike—1 or 2. Nike subcontracts its production to partners—that is where most hiring would take place under the Nike system. The local general/production manager would be free to do his own hiring.

6. In this company, the production schedule for each plant would need to be closely coordinated with the sales plan on an international basis.

Bata—1 or 2; Nike—4 or 5. Nike follows a strategy of outsourcing its production to cost efficient locations. Thus, its production centers would need to closely coordinate their activities with the sales efforts of the regions to which they ship. Bata's units are autonomous, mostly selling within the country they produce.

7. This company sees a need for clustering national units into regions for operational efficiencies. What would be the appropriate basis by which to undertake the restructuring?

Bata (geographic) would be more likely to cluster on a geographic basis since expatriates would build regional specialization, and training activities would be more relevant on a regional basis for similar countries. Nike (by product lines) is very product oriented and sees its athletes as similar across the globe in their use of a particular product be it soccer shoes or running shoes. Their operations would be clustered more by product lines.

8. A subsidiary of this company has identified a new line of footwear for use in schools in their physical education classes. Would prior permission be needed from the parent in order to proceed?

This is a subsidiary strategy issue. In the case of Bata, no permission would be needed. In the case of Nike, however, clearance from corporate office would need to be obtained, and such permission is not likely to be given unless the product can be launched elsewhere in a coordinated manner.

9. In the light of the responses to the above, what strategy would you say the company is following on an international plane?

This question concludes the discussion that began with the previous responses. Most students will identify that Bata follows a multidomestic strategy (which is how the company identifies itself in company literature) and Nike follows a global strategy. Multidomestic stands for low integration across country units and high local responsiveness. Global strategy stands for high integration and low responsiveness.

Both companies would be clustered between 2 and 4 on the five-point scale. The instructor can illustrate how in different ways both are global and multidomestic. Table 11.1 is useful for this purpose.

Table 11.1   Different Ways Bata and Nike Are Global and Multidomestic.

	Multidomestic	Global
Bata	Production scheduling, manufacturing, sourcing raw materials, distribution, ownership structure, some training, product development	Cost-leadership approach, factory and store designs, manufacturing methods
Nike	Retail channels, manufacturing arrangements	Focus differentiation strategy, marketing and promotion, product design, production scheduling, raw materials sourcing, distribution

It will be appropriate to point out that these are theoretical ends of a continuum and most companies fall somewhere along the line. The notion of "transnational strategy," advocated by Bartlett and Ghoshal, appears to be a relevant construct, which is a compromise. Transnational strategy attempts to combine high integration with high responsiveness. According to Bartlett and Ghoshal, in a transnational strategy, companies pursue several objectives simultaneously. They must exploit experience-based cost economies and location economies, transfer distinctive competencies within the company, and at the same time pay attention to pressures for local responsiveness. Since competencies can develop in any of the companies' operations, the flow of skills and product offerings can move from parent to subsidiary, from a subsidiary back to the parent, and between the subsidiaries.

10. Speculate on trends in the industry over the next ten years with respect to (a) consumer preferences for footwear, (b) national investment policies, and (c) any other. What changes would you recommend the company initiate in its strategy/operations to best face these trends, and why?

This is an open-ended question for a general discussion. Footwear is a subject that is close to the hearts of students, and they have varied—and definite—views on it. Students usually make several interesting comments on trends in this industry and how the companies should respond. Some comments on these trends include the increasing customization of athletic footwear by sport, function, color, and the like; and the move away from athletic footwear to more traditional leather-soled shoes for general purposes.

The instructor can raise the role of governments in influencing the transnational strategy choice of the firm. Nations have policies specifying governance/ownership structure (i.e., percentage of equity that can be held by foreigners), repatriation of profits, local employment policies, and so on. In the 1970s, for example, Coca-Cola preferred to exit the Indian market since it did not want to comply with local regulations requiring it to sell equity to the nationals. Similarly, in keeping with European Union regulations, some American companies set up significant activities like research and development in Europe to lend credence to their European subsidiaries being considered "local."

ASSESSMENT

For assessing this strategy session, have students respond to the following questions reproduced in the assessment form at the end of this session's instructor notes.

1. One company complained that its subsidiaries often withhold information because they consider the requests to be an infringement of their autonomy. What strategy is the parent company following?

   Answer: Could be either global or multidomestic. What this suggests is that neither the parent nor the subsidiary is clear about the strategy being followed. That can create several problems of control as the situation demonstrates.

2. It is necessary to have a global product in order to follow a global strategy. True or False?

Answer: False. While it makes it easier when the product is "global" such as Coca-Cola soft drinks, or Microsoft's Office Suite, there are several aspects to strategy apart from the product. Even when the product is a nonstandard one, such as automobiles, firms are moving towards a global strategy to take advantages from coordination of design, supplies, and production across nations.

3. In some companies, new capabilities and products are developed in both head office and overseas locations, independently and jointly. They are then transferred globally throughout the organization. What strategy is being followed here?

    Answer: A hybrid of global and multidomestc, referred to as a *transnational strategy.*

REFERENCES

Bartlett, Christopher A. and Sumantra Ghosal. 1989. *Managing Across Borders.* Boston: Harvard Business School Press.

Harzing, Anne-Wil. 2000. An empirical analysis and extension of the Bartlett and Ghosal typology of multinational companies. *Journal of International Business Studies* 31(1): 101–120.

Name:_____

ASSESSMENT FORM: STRATEGY SESSION 11

1. One company complained that its subsidiaries often withhold information because they consider the requests to be an infringement of their autonomy. What strategy is the parent company following?

_____

_____

_____

_____

_____

_____

2. It is necessary to have a global product in order to follow a global strategy. True or False?

_____

_____

_____

_____

_____

3. In some companies, new capabilities and products are developed in both head office and overseas locations, independently and jointly. They are then transferred globally throughout the organization. What strategy is being followed here?

_____

_____

_____

_____

_____

_____

Exercise: The Decline-Turnaround Sequence

OBJECTIVE

Students in this session develop an understanding of the critical issues surrounding organizational decline and the nature of turnaround management. Research into the nature of organizational decline reveals several patterns that organizations follow when they enter a stage of decline and failure. An understanding of these issues enables a manager to better understand the consequences of inaction and assist in developing a viable turnaround strategy.

Time: 70 minutes

ADMINISTRATION

Before Class

This exercise works well with teams of two to four students. Before the class session, instruct students to search databases such as ABI/Inform, Infotrac, Lexis/Nexis, and the like, with keywords such as "business failure" and "turnaround." (Web searches can also be employed.) Students should then identify an appropriate article using the following criteria:

- The article should be about one firm and be about three to four pages long.
- It should contain sufficient information, including the problems faced by the firm and what actions are being taken.
- The article should preferably be from one of the mainstream business magazines, such as *Business Week, Fortune, Fast Company, Forbes,* and *Inc.*

The team should make copies of the article for its team members. They should read the article before coming to class.

Another option is for the instructor to identify articles about corporations in decline-turnaround and assign them to the students.[*]

---

[*] For discussions of Xerox Corp., see Jeremy Kahn and Julie Schlosser. 2000. The paper jam from hell. *Fortune* (November 13) 142(11): 141–144; Peter Coy. 2000. The myth of corporate reinvention. *Business Week* (October 30) 3705: 80–82; and Pamela L. Moore. 2000. How Xerox ran short of black ink. *Business Week* (October 30) 3705: 56).

In Class

Instruct students to meet in their respective teams and discuss the article. They should look for information in the article to complete the exercise form in the student text (about 20 minutes). Instruct them to make entries on one form per team and turn it in at the end of class. (Two forms, reproduced in Figures 12.1 and 12.2, were completed in actual classes and serve as illustration for the instructor.)

DEBRIEFING

Debriefing should also take about 30 minutes. When the teams have completed their respective forms, the discussion commences. The instructor should go over the items in the form one by one. When each item is taken up for discussion, the instructor should first ask each team to report the information they have noted on their form. A wide and interesting range is usually available for the class to compare and comment upon. This is the reason for requiring students to identify their own cases for analysis, and it provides a variety in the class and allows for comparison on the context across different settings. The instructor then introduces the relevant concept, connects it to the information identified, and derives implications. The "answers" in the next section follow the questions in the students' forms, and can be used as part of the discussion.

1. Definition and extent of decline.

There will be a wide variety in the definitions of decline reported by the students in terms of falling sales, stock price, profitability, losses, and so on, and some discussion can flow from the implication of each definition. It may be pointed out to the students that the severity of decline arises when there is already a net loss consecutively over several quarters. Where the firm has not been facing losses but has been losing market share, realizing declining profits, or experiencing falling stock prices, the firm may be on a decline path; and these could be viewed as early indicators.

It is also useful to discuss whether the decline has been sudden or gradual, and the implications of the same. When the decline is gradual, the organization often adjusts to a low level of performance and stagnates there. Whether the firm is facing losses or just declining profits, there is a need for turnaround strategies in order to return to its former growth path.

2. What is the crisis? How was the decline recognized?

It is axiomatic that the earlier decline is recognized, the easier the turnaround. Quite often, the incumbent management has a tendency to delay recognition of decline, especially when it has been gradual. There are several reasons for this:

- Sometimes surprise-threatening information is rejected by managers as being too abstract, unreliable, or unrelated to past information.
- Commitment to a course of action results in information that the action is failing to be ignored.
- Or, due to "threat rigidity," there is a restriction in information processing and humans tend to rely on well rehearsed responses. They revert to "standard operating procedures: that do not solve the problem.

Management recognizes the severity of decline when it unwittingly faces a crisis. Some student teams will identify a takeover threat from another firm, banks putting pressure on the firm to protect their funds, a liquidity crisis, or a sudden exodus of key management personnel. All of these serve as triggers precipitating a crisis and forcing firms to initiate action.

3. Changes in the top management team (TMT).

In turnaround situations, there are usually changes in the top management team. The different reasons for this are:

- The existing management is held responsible for the decline.
- There is a need for a scapegoat.
- Or a symbolic act at this stage occurs to signify the onset of change.

Several writers have suggested that a change in top management is a necessary precondition for successful turnarounds.

Students usually find several instances of TMT changes, sometimes more than one in the same organization. The change could be dramatic and played out in the front pages of the business press, as we have seen in the cases of IBM, Compaq, General Motors, and so on. Empirical studies show considerable support for the view that new CEOs should be brought in to bring about a turnaround. Students' comments can be extracted on the style of the new team and how it contrasts with the previous CEO.

4. Complete the following table.

Causes for Decline   One of the first steps in turnaround management is to identify the causes for decline. Internal causes are usually the result of defects in top management or management errors of omission and commission. They include inefficient operations, lack of effective controls, over-expansion, and the like. External causes could be due to general economic conditions, competitive activity, and regulations.

Students find it easier to differentiate between internal and external causes for decline rather than strategic and operational causes. At this stage, the instructor must make the crucial distinction and ask the students to identify from among the causes already listed those they would consider as strategic. Discussion can also be held on the extent to which the external causes are external and if management could have taken steps to prevent or diminish the effect.

Turnaround Actions   At this stage, encourage the students to link the turnaround actions with the identified causes by drawing arrows on the form. The appropriate turnaround strategy would be the one that tackles the causes of decline. Connecting the turnaround actions with the causes can be very revealing because it becomes very clear to students how obviously the two should be related but often are not. This can be due to poor design of the turnaround, or more importantly, difficulty in arriving at the several causes for decline.

At this time, ask students which of the steps are strategic and which are operational. Broadly, strategic steps would involve repositioning the company, giving it a new direction, and divestment moves. Operational steps would be related to improving efficiency within the organization such as raising productivity and cutting costs. It is important to stress that if the strategic causes are not tackled, the turnaround is short lived. Strategic problems cannot be solved by operational efficiencies.

The question of severity can be addressed by separating steps taken to stem the decline by improving cash flow. These actions produce immediate results such as asset reduction strategies (sale of assets to raise cash), layoffs, cost cutting, and reducing inventories. Once decline has been stemmed, revenue-generating strategies would be initiated that take longer to show results and involve expenditures. These include new product development, marketing efforts, and so on.

At this stage, instructors can pause for ten minutes and give the teams time to identify actions they feel the company should take in light of the above discussion.

Stakeholders   When a firm is in decline, the TMT is rarely exempt from the influence of other stakeholders who begin to see a threat to their stake in the firm and want to be involved in the turnaround process. A discussion of the role of these stakeholders brings home the point that management does not have exclusive control over a turnaround situation and has to depend on other agencies. For instance, the need for additional funding to finance turnaround efforts requires the cooperation of the bank, which may stipulate certain conditions that would require changes in the turnaround strategy. Suppliers would demand payment and need to be co-opted to extend payment terms and thereby help the firm. Each stakeholder would try to influence the organization to suit its own needs, which can result in contradictory pressures.

Results   A discussion of the results of the actions initiated would conclude the exercise by evaluating the success of actions initiated. This part can also be tied into the definition of decline to see if the same measures are used.

ASSESSMENT

The completed form may be collected and assigned a grade based on: (a) the extent to which the information has been transcribed onto the form; and (b) the quality and relevance of items entered into the causes and turnaround actions columns. While the students are discussing and completing the form, the instructor can walk around the class, observe the discussion, and take notes to help in grading individuals and teams for the quality of the discussion. Examples based on actual class sessions follow. The example tables reproduced in Figures 12.1 and 12.2 illustrate results that can be used as a guideline when you explain the form in the class.

Example 1   Apple Corp. (Period of decline: 1995-1998)*

1. *Definition and extent of the decline:* Loss of $2 billion between 1995–1998. Market share dropped from 9% to 2.5%.
2. *Crisis:* (How decline was recognized?) Falling market share and income. Huge drop in market value shocked the firm.
3. *Changes in TMT:* Fired most of the board; CEO Gil Amelio terminated; Steve Jobs hired to manage company's recovery.

---

* Students used the following articles for this exercise: David Kirkpatrick. 1998. The second coming of Apple. *Fortune* (November 9) 138(9): 86–92; and Peter Burrows. 1997. A peek at Steve Jobs' plan. *Business Week* (November 17) 3553: 144–146.

4. *Table:* See Figure 12.1.
5. *Results:* The stock price has increased from $12.75 to $37. Profit has increased.

Example 2   Club Med (Period of decline: 1994–1997)*

1. *Definition and extent of the decline:* Decline in profits, stock price and revenues. Losses of $230 million in 1997.
2. *Crisis:* (How decline was recognized?) Announcement of loss for 1996 of $130 million instead of an expected profit of $ 40 million shocked stockholders.
3. *Changes in TMT:* Fired CEO and several top executives.
4. *Table:* See Figure 12.2.
5. *Results:* Stock price increasing and income also showing signs of increasing.

Figure 12.1   Apple Corp.—Causes of Decline.

Cause of Decline:	Turnaround Actions:
External	*Strategic*
1. Fewer software vendors.	1. Eliminating unfocused products.
2. Loss of court case on patents.	2. Identifying its loyal market segment and serving them.
3. Competition from Microsoft with new Windows system, and high installed base of software.	3. Alliance with Microsoft for developing software.
	4. Launch of iMac.
Internal	*Operational*
1. Shortage of products during periods of strong demand.	1. Direct sales via Internet.
2. Loss of product identity.	2. Liquidating inventories.
3. Large inventories when demand dried up.	3. New marketing efforts to re-build brand; Increased advertising.
4. Inability to adapt to changing market.	
5. Product not differentiated from Wintel.	
Stakeholders Involved:	**Their Role:**
1. Apple loyalists/education and publishing markets.	1. Demanding changes and action be taken while attending conferences.
2. Stockholders.	2. Demanding changes.

---

* Students used the following article for this exercise: Celia Daurat. 1999. Paradise regained. *Forbes* (March 22) 163(6): 102–104.

Figure 12.2   Club Med—Causes of Decline

Cause of Decline:	Turnaround Actions:
External	*Strategic*
1. Changes in social preferences, customer needs and tastes.	1. New product offerings and similar pricing for all customers.
2. Poor image among family clientele.	2. Change of image to "wholesome."
Internal	*Operational*
1. Poor upkeep of properties.	1. $300 million renovation campaign.
2. Bureaucracy and slow decision making.	2. Working with travel agencies to attract groups.
	3. Closing unprofitable units.
	4. Downsizing.
Stakeholders Involved:	**Their Role:**
FIAT automobile family, large stockholders.	Forced CEO to resign.

Strategy Session 13

Succeeding in Strategy Formulation and Implementation

Exercise: Diagnosing Problems at Procter & Gamble

OBJECTIVE

This strategy session highlights for students the importance of formulation and implementation for a successful strategy.

Time: 30–60 minutes

ADMINISTRATION

The exercise is designed to help students diagnose organizational problems from a strategic perspective. This is accomplished by comparing what a company said it was going to do (its strategy) versus how it has executed that strategy (implementation). Students can perform this exercise individually or in teams. The exercise takes 30 minutes if prepared individually in class for the first 15 minutes and then discussed in the remaining time. If performed in teams, allow 30 minutes for team preparation and another 30 minutes for class presentation and discussion.

The formulation/implementation matrix is a useful tool for diagnosing problems presented in case studies or for analyzing actual company situations that students may be required to do in out-of-class projects.

The reading and exercise should make two things clear:

- Strategy implementation is at least as important as strategy formulation. Unfortunately, when developing strategies, managers are inclined to assume that effective implementation will occur. It should be obvious, however, that what organizations actually do is at least as important as what they plan to do.
- The quality of a formulated strategy is difficult if not impossible to assess in the absence of effective implementation. Diagnosing organizational problems requires analysis of both formulation and implementation.

If time permits, the class might discuss the new CEO's plan to reconsider new product launches already on the calendar (modify strategy formulation) and to reverse the trend of changing too much, too fast (modify strategy implementation). The danger with this plan to do things in the more traditional Procter & Gamble way is that it may be a short-term fix and will not likely be the answer to the bottom-line problems that have plagued the company for the last ten years.

DEBRIEFING

In the exercise, students analyze the formulation and implementation of a strategy. The debriefing can center on the questions answered individually or in teams.

1. Describe the strategy developed for Procter & Gamble by Jager. Was it a strong or weak strategy? (To determine if the strategy was strong or weak, review whether it dealt with environmental trends and whether it would offset company weaknesses or capitalize upon company strengths.)

    The Jager strategy can be described as an aggressive growth strategy that focused on gaining global market share through speed and innovation. It consisted of ambitious new product launches, a global orientation, and acquisitions in order to achieve large gains in market share. This was his formula for P&G growth. He rightfully realized that the company could not cost-cut itself to prosperity and thus set aggressive sales targets. However, boosting sales means boosting expenses, and when sales did not grow as fast as expected, profits suffered.

    This strategy capitalized on P&G's strengths in brand recognition (e.g., Tide, Ivory, Pampers) in the global marketplace, as well as its strong presence in supermarket distribution. It also was designed to offset company weaknesses of a risk averse culture and slow responses to customers. Similar to many organizations during the late 1980s and 1990s, the company had become so focused on internal cost efficiencies that it paid less attention to increasing market share, particularly on a global basis. Jager's strategy was designed to offset the company's rigid structure and a roster of old-line, slow-growing products.

2. Identify ways the strategy was implemented. Was it executed well? Discuss.

    New product development: Jager increased funding for research and development. He eliminated a rigid budget process that involved lengthy reviews and presentations that were part of the product development process. He instituted "stretch goals," where a business segment could spend based on its targeted sales. This resulted in businesses overspending and helped contribute to costs rising more than sales.

    Acquisitions: The Iams dog food acquisition was implemented well. P&G took this $800 million private brand and shipped it to its vast array of supermarket customers. Market share grew by taking this high-margin, high-turn business to the mass market. However, a botched attempt at acquiring Gillette Co. was costly, and pressures from investors caused Jager to abort the high-risk acquisition of Warner-Lambert Co. and American Home Products Corp

    Corporate culture and politics: Perhaps the most critical implementation problem occurred because of Jager's leadership style. Lower management balked at his brusqueness. E-mails and letters from midlevel managers began circulating, complaining about morale and a lack of confidence in his leadership. As Jager preached rebellion, management became frustrated as they moved away from by-the-book procedures.

Reorganizations: Jager reorganized the old-fashioned international network of 144 regional managers and reorganized the company into seven global business units built around product lines. The process broke up decades-old fiefdoms and gave P&G the ability to respond more quickly and efficiently to global trends. However, in those same e-mails, some managers complained they did not know who was responsible for what.

Today, CEOs face tough times, and the penalty for failure is coming more swiftly than in previous decades. Coca-Cola Co.'s M. Douglas Ivester, who quit after two years on the job, built his reputation as an aggressive operator who made brassy but ill-fated acquisition moves (trying to buy Pernod Ricard SA's Orangina brand and Cadbury Schweppes PLC's overseas beverage business) shortly after taking the top job. His steamroller style, insensitivity to politics and the CocaCola culture, and the company's poor earnings led to his downfall.

3. In Figure 13.2, place an "X" in the cell that best depicts the Procter & Gamble situation.

Draw the matrix on the board. Then, ask each team or each student to identify where in the matrix they placed Procter and Gamble. Most students will put the "X" in the lower left cell. Occasionally, some students will argue that the chosen strategy was also not a strong one, and therefore the "X" would be placed in the lower right cell. However, these students should be asked to justify their diagnosis of the strategy based on environmental conditions. Clearly, revenue growth must be achieved if the company expects to increase profits, since cost cutting measures can only improve the bottom line for so long.

Possible solution to Figure 13.2 in student text.

	Strategy Formulation	
	Strong	**Weak**
Strong		
Weak	X	

Strategy Implementation

ASSESSMENT

The assessment form at the end these instructor notes for this exercise is given to students on an individual basis after the exercise is finished. The questions are similar to those given in the exercise, with the exception of the first question, which asks students to identify the specific strategy developed for Procter & Gamble. Possible responses follow:

1. What was the corporate-level strategy developed for Procter & Gamble by Jager?

    The strategy was an aggressive growth strategy through acquisitions and internal development to increase global market share.

2. Was it a strong or a weak strategy? Briefly discuss. To determine if the strategy was strong or weak, review whether it dealt with environmental trends and whether it would offset company weaknesses or capitalize upon company strengths.

    The strategy was good. It dealt with environmental trends, particularly the saturated American market and strong global population growth. It also offset the company's weakness of relying on cost cutting itself to prosperity. The strategy also was designed to move P&G away from its image of being stodgy and an "Old Economy" company.

3. Identify ways the strategy was implemented. Was it executed well? Discuss.

    - **The R&D process was revamped and executed well. It allowed P&G to bring products to market faster.**
    - **The acquisition of IAMS proved successful; however, the Gillette Co. acquisition attempt was costly and caused investors to become apprehensive when the high-risk acquisition of Warner Lambert Co. and American Home Products Corp. was proposed by Jager.**
    - **The reorganization of the company into seven global business units made sense; however, it was executed poorly. The reorganizations confused and demoralized the employees.**

4. Based on your discussion above, place an "X" in the box that best depicts the Procter & Gamble situation.

Strategy Formulation

		Strong	Weak
	Strong		
Strategy Implementation	**Weak**	**X**	

Name: _____

ASSESSMENT FORM: STRATEGY SESSION 13

1. What was the corporate-level strategy developed for Procter & Gamble by Jager?

_____

_____

_____

_____

_____

2. Was it a strong or a weak strategy? Briefly discuss. To determine if the strategy was strong or weak, review whether it dealt with environmental trends and whether it would offset company weaknesses or capitalize upon company strengths.

_____

_____

_____

_____

_____

3. Identify ways the strategy was implemented. Was it executed well? Discuss.

_____

_____

_____

_____

_____

_____

_____

4. Based on your discussion above, place an "X" in the box that best depicts the Procter & Gamble situation.

Strategy Formulation

		Strong	Weak
Strategy Implementation	**Strong**		
	Weak		

Strategy Session 14

Structuring to Support Strategy

Exercise: Designing Organizational Structures for Club Ed

OBJECTIVE

In this session, students practice designing new structures and systems for a business as its strategy evolves.

Time: 90 minutes

ADMINISTRATION

The exercise—a team activity—requires students to work in small groups of three to five individuals. The materials required are three overhead transparency blanks and markers for each group of students.

The groups will design the structure and systems of a resort business as it grows from one location to 50 different sites and diversifies over a period of 20 years.

Instructors can make the exercise more or less complex by only focusing on structural transformations and ignoring systems design, examining questions related to running businesses in diverse cultures, emphasizing strategic decisions and their structure and design implications, and exploring their own particular views of the most relevant determinants of structure and design.

The exercise follows the evolution of the resort as it grows. This growth has been subdivided into three periods.

Period I (initial resort is established)

- 20 minutes for groups to identify their strategy and draw the organizational structure.
- 15 minutes for one or two groups to present their designs and lead class discussion.

Strategy

Most students describe their intended generic strategy as focused differentiation, targeting one group of customers. For example, a target segment might be families, college students, swinging singles, or business people. Occasionally a group identifies their intended generic strategy as broad differentiation (appealing to a wide customer base that includes many different market segments). However, it is a challenge to appeal to market segments with different life styles (for example, families and college students), and a brief discussion about this challenge can illustrate the advantages of a focus market scope.

Groups will describe various points on which to differentiate the resort. Some choose distinctive resort features, such as "gym suites," where an exercise machine (treadmill, bike, or StairMaster®) is located in every suite. Others pick location, such as a resort that offers ocean views from every room.

Structure

Students may draw a *simple* organizational structure with all 15 employees reporting directly to the owner or a slightly advanced design where some of the employees are grouped into *functions*. For example, the employees who work in operations may be grouped together (front desk, housekeeping, maintenance). Instructors can ask students if they have visited a resort to describe their experiences and spend some time brainstorming jobs and tasks. A detailed discussion of what functions should be included is beneficial because students underestimate the number of different functions that an organization of this type needs.

The teams' organizational structures will vary depending on the strategy chosen. For example, one group that chooses to differentiate based on its health club-type services (spas, massages, daily exercise classes, and so on) may create a separate fitness department as part of its organizational structure.

At this first stage, students usually omit a board of directors, which can lead to a brief exploration of governance, ownership, and stakeholder issues. The discussion, however, generally focuses on the functional approach to organizational structure and its advantages. Although discussion questions have been included in the exercise for each period to focus students' attention on issues to explore, these can be amended or replaced with questions more suited to the instructor's purposes. For example, the following can be asked at each stage:

- What type of structure have you drawn?
- Why is it appropriate?
- What problems are trying to address with this structure?
- How does this structure relate to your strategy?

Period II (ten years later—30 Club Eds)

- Reconvene groups. Allow 20 minutes for the groups to review the strategy, brainstorm problem areas, and develop the structure for their growing companies.
- 10 minutes for group presentation and class discussion.

To begin, ask one group to present its design and then ask if anyone did it differently.

Strategy

Two levels of strategy may be discussed. At the corporate level, a growth strategy resulted in 30 properties that are part of the Club Ed organization. This may have involved acquisition of properties, mergers, or resorts that the company built using internal funds. At the business level, some groups identify the same generic strategy at all 30 locations. For example, all properties may follow the first resort's differentiation strategy. That is, if the first resort was differentiated based on the exercise theme, with gym suites, trainers, and workout facilities, and then all 30 resorts might have the same theme. The advantages are shared resources and a strong identity for the organization. However, the disadvantage is that the company is vulnerable if exercise and fitness trends wane or if demographics change. Other designs may include different generic strategies for different properties.

Structure

Students may create a *functional* structure, with a president or chief executive officer, vice presidents of the functional groups (marketing, human resources, customer services, finance, operations—a managerial layer—and the line staff. Or they can design a *divisional* structure, in which resorts are grouped together based on geographic locations (one division for the Caribbean, one for North and South America, one for the South Pacific, and so on). Another possibility is a *hybrid* structure to meet the needs of geographic diversity or market segmentation. A hybrid design, for example, might have some functions centralized, such as finance, human resources, and marketing, and other functions, such as operations and customer service, repeated in each of the geographic divisions.

The discussion should focus on control versus autonomy, training and culture as adjuncts to structure, size as a structural determinant, and the strategy-structure link.

Period III (ten years later—50 clubs and three cruise ships)

- Reconvene groups. Allow 15 minutes for students to identify the new strategy and prepare the organizational chart.
- 10 minutes for group presentations.

Strategy

The discussion should focus primarily on corporate strategy in Period III. Most students identify it as related diversification, since the organization's effective resort operations management and its customer service expertise in the resort industry can be put to good use in the cruise industry. As the business moves to the next stage of its development, the emphasis is on the generation of issues and on the relationship of structure to strategy, size, environment, culture, job design, and systems design.

Structure

The corporate strategy favors an SBU structure, where resorts and cruise ships are two separate strategic business units. However, some students may suggest a type of network structure, where the company outsources some functions, such as marketing and information technology, instead of maintaining departments for these functions. This allows the organization to concentrate on its distinctive competencies (for example, resort operations and customer service), while gathering efficiencies from other firms that are concentrating their efforts in their areas of expertise.

To stimulate discussion, the instructor could ask if diversification into casinos or a travel agency chain, instead of cruise ships, would make a difference to the structure.

A discussion on the evolution of organizational design concludes and summarizes the exercise.

ASSESSMENT: DIRECTED PARAPHRASING

Directed paraphrasing is an assessment technique that provides feedback on the ability of students to summarize and restate important concepts in their own words. It allows faculty to assess how well students have understood and internalized the learning of the concepts. The fact that the paraphrase is "directed," aimed at a specific audience for a specific reason, makes the paraphrasing task more demanding and more useful than simple restatements. Copy the assignment below on the board or on an overhead slide and pass out half sheets of paper to students. Remind students to include their names and only two paragraphs of information.

Paraphrasing Assignment

Your Name:_____

You have just joined a company as assistant to the President. The company has grown to ten stores across the state, and it is following the same organizational structure it had when the company was started with one large store. In two paragraphs, paraphrase what organizational structure is and why it is critical that the President consider changes to the company's structure.

Once you have collected the written feedback, separate the responses into four piles, which might be labeled "confused," "minimal," "adequate," and "excellent." These assess the responses by comparing them within and across categories. Pay particular attention to three items:

- The accuracy of the paraphrase
- Its suitability for the intended audience
- Its effectiveness in fulfilling the assigned purpose.

Provide handouts with examples of particularly successful paraphrases. Be sure to pick an example or examples where the student has been particularly original. (Students, unfortunately, have had many years of practice in not writing in their own words.) If time permits, give each student a checklist of the strong and weak points of his or her response.

Strategy Session 15

Strategy Implementation Using the 7-S Model

Exercise: Transition at PeopleSoft Inc.

OBJECTIVE

Students in this session recognize the actions needed in different areas of the organization in order to implement strategy and to appreciate the interrelationships of the actions.

Time: 60 minutes

ADMINISTRATION

The exercise may be administered on an individual basis or as a group exercise in two phases.

Phase I (20 minutes)

Administering the exercise on an individual basis   Instruct students to read the case PeopleSoft and follow the instructions in the exercise before coming to class—that is, identify the data pertaining to the items of the 7-S model and complete the "current" portion of the boxes. In class, form the students into groups and ask them to build a consensus on the 7-S's. Their task as a team is to identify if the actions currently being taken by PeopleSoft in each of the boxes support their strategy.

Administering the exercise as a group exercise   Instruct students to only read the case before coming to class. In class, first assign to each student one or two of the S's on which to focus. Have the students identify examples from the case that would fit into the boxes provided describing elements of the 7-S model. Next, ask students to move around the class and form teams so that all the S's are represented in each team. Their task as a team is to identify if the actions currently being taken by PeopleSoft in each of the boxes support their strategy.

Phase II (15 minutes)

Make copies of the "Update" provided in the appendix in these instructor notes for this session and distribute it to the students. As a team, the students should identify what changes they would like to make in light of the new information. These are to be entered in the boxes under "Recommendations."

DEBRIEFING

Allot 25 minutes for debriefing. The follow notes can form the basis for discussion.

Background to McKinsey Model

This exercise is based on the McKinsey 7-S model. The model was used extensively by the McKinsey consulting firm as a way of thinking broadly about the problems of effective organizations. T. J. Peters and R. H. Waterman's best-selling book *In Search of Excellence* (New York: Harper & Row, 1982) is based on the principles underlying this model. The popularity of the model declined when some of the companies deemed excellent in the book, such as IBM and Hewlett-Packard, stumbled along the way. Using additional criteria, academics also questioned the classification of some of the companies as excellent. This model, however, is intuitively appealing and has remained a fixture in many strategy textbooks to illustrate the many facets of an organization that are involved in strategy implementation. More recently, Senge, in his work, also draws inspiration from the 7-S as a way of explaining change in organizations.

The 7-S model suggests that (a) a multiplicity of factors affect an organization's success; (b) all of them need to be aligned and support each other; and (c) there is no start or finish to the model. The elements are equally important though at different times, one or more may be critical to the organization.

As students report the entries in each box, ask them to comment on whether it connects with the content in any other box. These connections stress the interrelationships in the decisions taken to implement strategy. The following sections discuss each of the S's. Figure 15.1 provides a completed form as a guide for the instructor.

Superordinate Goals

Another way of viewing this item is to think of it as "shared values." These values may go beyond simple goal statements and are shared widely by the employees of the company. Values repeatedly mentioned by both CEOs include retaining a strong employee-based culture, innovation, and customer service.

Strategy

The company's strategy is in transition. From being focused on the upper-end ERP market, the slowing down of the industry is forcing it into e-commerce applications, which is a rapidly growing business. Meanwhile, other players are moving into the midmarket (which is an important segment for PeopleSoft and is a segment with a new entrant, J. D. Edwards). E-commerce is also attracting others into the ERP industry. For this reason, it is important that PeopleSoft carve out its niche carefully.

PeopleSoft's strategy now should be to maintain its market share in the ERP market and grow in new areas such as the Web. Yet, on the Web, strategies change rapidly, sometimes as quickly as every quarter. Other options are to examine their existing customer base (companies to which they have supplied ERP software) and extend products to them. Another alternative is a portal on the Web with built-in software to enable firms to manage their performance using the tools of ERP.

Structure

What kind of structure would suit an organization like this? As the firm moves into a new strategy, it needs to create new divisions for the ERP and e-commerce activities. Even within this initiative, questions such as whether the sales organization should be client-based or product-based must be decided. In addition, the company must consider mechanisms that can be put in place to ensure integration among the various groups in the organization (for example, cross-functional teams of designers in the human resources area and designers in the manufacturing area).

Systems

Software companies usually have few rigid systems. This is true especially for firms that are operating on the Web. Yet, as firms grow, they also need more formalized planning. As the PeopleSoft case illustrates, lack of proper environmental scanning made the slowing down of the ERP industry come as a surprise. PeopleSoft also needs to be more mature in dealing with the press, Wall Street analysts, and other external parties, since this type of interaction is expected of a billion-dollar company. Recall that the replacement of founder Steve Jobs as CEO by Sculley in the early days of Apple was for a similar purpose—that is; to bring stability and systems into the company. It is easier to manage mergers and acquisitions with well-established systems.

Style

Culture of a start-up usually molds itself around the founder, as in this case. This has been institutionalized by several practices and is now widely shared. Clearly, the fun atmosphere is a fundamental strength and needs to be protected. The question is how to bring accountability with this? The continuance of Duffield as Chairman ensures the culture is protected, which is a condition under which Conway would have to operate.

Staff

Morale has been affected by the layoffs. In addition, falling stock prices would affect those who are holding stock options. Also, when a firm moves from a rapid growth to slow or flat growth, it affects the attitudes of those employees who would like to be working on cutting-edge technologies and products and may therefore want to leave.

New skills for the organization in the areas of Web commerce need to be built by recruiting the right kind of people. In addition, giving technology-driven high performers the option to move into new e-commerce areas help retain their interest.

Skills

Clearly, the background of Conway suggests that he has the expertise of the new Web-based businesses towards which the company is moving. In addition, the company might consider acquiring a new firm in this business.

Figure 15.1   7-S Model Using the PeopleSoft Paradigm

Superordinate Goals (Guiding concepts, a set of values and aspirations, often unwritten that may go beyond formally stated objectives. They are succinct, abstract, and mean a lot to insiders.)

Current actions:

Having fun while working in the company and running a people-sensitive enterprise. Being a leader in innovation, quality, and customer service.

Recommendations:

Make accountability an all-pervading issue—organization to be goal and task oriented without sacrificing the fun.

Strategy (Actions planned in response to or in anticipation of changes in the external environment—customers and competition)

Current actions:

Pioneer in ERP industry; widen the range of applications offered while increasing the company's dominance in the midmarket.

Recommendations:

Maintaining position in the ERP industry, without seeking to increase share, while expanding into new applications to serve the e-commerce market. Seek specific niches in e-commerce such as small organizations, companies in specific industries, or business-to-business.

Structure (The division of tasks and its coordination within the company)

Current actions:

Flat organization, with minimum of bureaucracy.

Recommendations:

Integrate acquisitions more quickly by eliminating duplications in activities. Create divisions for ERP and e-commerce. Decide on a client-based sales organization, for example, that could be shared by both organizations.

Systems (All the procedures, formal and informal, that make the organization work: budgeting systems, training systems, accounting systems, etc.)

Current actions:

Few formal systems implied (forgiveness rather than permission). Empowered to make decisions.

Recommendations:

Set goals in product development. Regular environment scanning systems, scenario building.

Figure 15.1   7-S Model Using the PeopleSoft Paradigm (cont.)

Style (A representation of the organization's culture, it reflects the values and beliefs as demonstrated in symbolic behavior)
Current actions:
Informal and sensitive. Theme park-like atmosphere. Casual dress.
Recommendations:
Maintain casual atmosphere but institute some accountability, such as goal-based management systems (MBO) and incentive programs tied to goal achievement.
Staff (The people issues, both hard—pay scales, training programs, etc.— and soft—morale, attitude, motivation, etc.)
Current actions:
Family-friendly policies. Good benefits, flexible work rules, employee stock ownership plan. High morale and motivation, now suffering with increasing turnover.
Recommendations:
Need to boost morale by declaring end of layoffs. Allow employees to shift voluntarily to e-commerce activities, if desired. Offer higher stock options based on tenure to reduce turnover and the like. Recruit new people with e-commerce skills.
Skills (Crucial attributes of the company, its strengths, and competencies)
Current actions:
High levels of customer service. Knowledge and information about integrating activities in a varied range of enterprises.
Recommendations:
ERP required dealing with other large businesses. E-commerce may involve dealing with several small and start-up businesses.

ASSESSMENT

While the students in each team may have made notes on individual forms, ask them to have one complete form ready per team for collection at the end of class. Evaluate using the following criteria:

1. If the students have correctly identified data for all the S's.
2. If they see the change in strategy as needing changes in other areas of the organization.

   Grade the assignment so that all members receive the team grade.

Strategy Session 15 Appendix: PeopleSoft Update

In early 1999, PeopleSoft went through a period of layoffs that most people thought would never happen in the "family." Managers agonized about it. Some wept in departmental meetings while planning how to conduct the layoffs. When 430 employees were laid off, some were informed over voicemail, others were not given any explanation, and one employee was called in the middle of her vacation and told not to return. Yet, in a company chatroom, postings did not generate expressions of anger or frustration from current or departing employees, just support for the company and Duffield. The employee turnover rate that used to be barely five percent a year now stands at 20 percent. Employee defections have intensified as workers seek greener pastures with technology start-ups.

Craig Conway, who joined PeopleSoft in mid-1999 as President, was appointed CEO by the end of the year. Before joining PeopleSoft, he was chief executive for OneTouch Systems, a leader in interactive broadcast networks and distance learning. Previously, he had served as chief executive for TGV Software, Inc., an early developer of network protocols and applications for corporate intranets and the Internet. Conway has also spent eight years at Oracle Corporation in a variety of roles including marketing, sales, and operations.

Conway was perhaps the only man who wore a tie, but he promised that the casual dress code and egalitarianism would remain. He said he would bring "mature management," "predictability," and "accountability" to the company. Commenting on Conway's appointment as CEO, Duffield noted that the culture lacked accountability. He felt that the company needed people who committed to something and then got it done and said Conway could achieve that.

While pursuing the same overall strategy as its competitors, Conway says he will focus on providing more innovative technology, greater flexibility, faster implementation, lower costs and better customer support than PeopleSoft's rivals. In addition, the company has large growth plans in the areas of e-commerce and software systems for smaller companies. Conway commented, "I am absolutely committed to upholding the values that Dave has instilled in the company, including its strong employee culture and its reputation as a respected, trusted partner."

Duffield remains as Chairman of the Board. He will continue to take part in strategic decisions and spend time building relationships with customers and employees. He will also promote the core values that inspire PeopleSoft's culture as a leader in innovation, quality, and customer service.

With ERP slowing, other markets are looking attractive. The American business-to-consumer and business-to-business e-commerce markets are scheduled to grow to $108 billion and $1.3 trillion respectively by 2003. ERP vendors are rushing to build e-commerce applications on a backbone with which they are already familiar. These applications would stretch across the enterprise as a whole, with links into inventory management, production planning, the sales ledger and distribution planning. Oracle and SAP have announced business-to-business portals.

PeopleSoft's goal is to be a provider of e-commerce applications and has recently released PeopleSoft 8, consisting of 100 percent Web-based technology and applications. Conway admits that Oracle is six months ahead in its e-commerce deployment, but he is confident that PeopleSoft can catch up.

Strategy Session 16

The Role of Cooperation in Strategic Management

Exercise: Acting Out the Commons' Dilemma*

OBJECTIVE

Students in this session learn to recognize the areas of cooperation that exist even within a competitive market economy. They will also appreciate the individual skills required to cooperate with other firms.

Time: 75–120 minutes

ADMINISTRATION

The time frame for this session's exercise is somewhat elastic. The first phase of the exercise takes about 15 minutes. The second phase is *expandable*, and the number of rounds played depends on the time available. The number of rounds must be announced at the start of this phase. A minimum of five rounds is recommended which should take about eight minutes each. Debriefing for about ten minutes is recommended after each phase.

Phase I

The students may complete this individually or in groups of three or four as convenient. Ask them to identify areas in the business environment where there is need for firms, in the same industry or across different industries, to cooperate. They may be asked to list the reasons for each instance of cooperation they are able to identify.

At the end of the scheduled time, call upon individuals or groups, in turn, to report to the class an instance of cooperation that they have listed and the reasons identified. Encourage others to comment on the items being reported as to whether they agree or disagree. The objective is to get the students to identify the reasons why a particular cooperative activity is taking place and thereby appreciate the pre-conditions for the same. The discussion below provides the instructor with background information. The purpose of this phase is to clarify in the minds of the students that extensive cooperation does take place in various forms, so they are prepared to seriously participate in the second phase.

---

* Adapted from Gary M. Throop. 1989. All managers have a commons (sic) problem: Instruction effects vs. payoff structure in a commons dilemma situation. Paper presented at the Eastern Academy of Management Annual Meeting, Portland, Maine, May 1989. Used with permission.

Debriefing

Several factors determine the nature of cooperative arrangements. These include: horizontal or vertical relationships (the positions of the firms in the value chain), whether the time frame is short- or long-term, whether it is limited to one product/market combination or to many, and whether it affects only one subset of the activities of the company or is company-wide. Different combinations of these factors may reveal different kinds of cooperation that takes place in the business environment. The following is a partial list of some categories that we can observe, and which would be familiar to the students:

1. **Industry structure**   The nature of the industry structure may require firms to compete and cooperate at the same time. Ray Noorda, founder of the software company Novell, is credited with coining the term "co-opetition" to describe this situation. Brandenburgher and Nalebuff rely on game theory to model a framework that builds this notion of co-opetition. Their model, called "Value Net," suggests that there are five players in a "business game": Apart from the company, there are the customers, suppliers, and competitors—to which they add a fifth called "complementors." A player is a complementor if consumers value a company's product more when they have the complementor's product than when they have the company's product alone. A player is a competitor if customers value the company's product less when they have the competitor's product. For example, French's is a complementor of Oscar Meyer since consumers of hot dogs value Oscar Meyer more when they have French's mustard than when they do not. (And, by turns, Oscar Meyer is a complementor to French's.) The idea that there are competitors and complementors to a firm therefore suggests that the firm, at the same time, is cooperating with some and competing with others.

2. **Setting standards**   Product or technology standards are often required for a market to grow rapidly. In some cases, a regulatory body or a single dominant firm may set the standard (for example, Microsoft's operating system). More commonly, firms may join into one or more standard setting alliances. For example, the VHS alliance was coordinated by Matsushita to establish a video recorder standard. In the UNIX alliance, rival competing alliances formed to strive for a standard. When there are no standards, the cost to the consumer of adopting such products are high and consumer interest is low. Therefore, it is in the interest of the producers to develop such standards through cooperation.

3. **Basic research**   Cooperation can be undertaken by firms that do not directly compete if there are benefits in sharing the outcome of expensive basic research. Sometimes, even direct competitors can cooperate to develop a new design of a product from which both benefit. An example of this is the collaboration by Fuji and Kodak, companies that both manufacture camera film, along with Canon, Nikon, and Minolta, companies that produce cameras, to develop the new "smart film" technology. Fuji and Kodak have almost 80% market share in Japan and the U.S. and are collaborating from positions of strength. The collaboration not only helped develop the technology but also simultaneously developed a standard that others would now have to follow. IBM cooperates with rivals Toshiba and Siemens to develop memory chips.

4. **Strategic alliance**   This is a particular instance of collaboration that is gaining increasing popularity. See Strategy Session 10 on strategic alliances.

5. **The Commons dilemma**   The "Tragedy of the Commons" is a particular instance of the more generic issue of what is called the "Prisoner's Dilemma" in the field of game theory. The basic idea is that individual self-interest (maximizing one's individual utility) can lead to the overexploitation of a common resource with the result that the resource will be destroyed over time. A traditional example of this is the use of the village commons for the grazing of animals. In modern times, we see a similar situation arising in polluted regions, whereby individual polluters try cut costs by not installing pollution-control equipment—however, the deterioration of air quality affects everybody. It also applies to the case of restricting fishing in an area in order to protect the total fish stock. Oil drillers face the same situation when they are sharing a *common* pool of oil resources. Without restrictions that prevent overfishing, the fishing fleets of different nations will maximize their individual utility functions to the detriment of the fisheries that are, in effect, their "commons." Thus, there is a need for cooperation by individuals in order to protect the general environment (economic or ecological) within which they compete.

A general concluding point that may be stressed to students is that for firms to enter into a cooperative arrangement, there often must be the conviction of an economic benefit to them individually that would arise from cooperation.

Phase II

In Phase I, the focus was on cooperation among organizations. This phase takes students to the next stage of translating the concept of cooperation into individual behavior. It is important to stress this distinction when introducing Phase II to the students. In the reading, students learn about the value net and its concept of complementor. A complementor may or may not cooperate with the firm producing the product it complements. In this phase, students are led through a process that makes them reflect on what it takes, at an individual level, to cooperate. When firms cooperate, it requires individuals on both sides to be comfortable with the notion of cooperation. Since we are from early childhood brought up with the notion of competing for success, cooperating requires a reframing of the situation or the problem. It requires a development of conviction in the broader goals of the activity, and the development of trust in relation to the competitor in order to move into a position of cooperation.

At the beginning of this phase of the exercise, the instructor needs to:

1. Remind students that they will act in an individual capacity. Only the instructor will know their decision—the other students will not know.
2. Determine and announce the number of rounds the game is played. A minimum of five is recommended.
3. Provide students with some incentive to get involved. The payoff matrix, explained below, provides a calculation of points that each student earns in the game. The instructor may translate the points earned by the participants towards a grade. (At the very least, a bar of chocolate may be offered to the high scorers!)

The payoff matrix is constructed so that the competor gets more points than the cooperator, as long as there are both categories in class.

Cooperator's score	90% – [(90% / Number students) x Number of competors]
Competor's score	Cooperator's score + 10%

The construction of the matrix is such that if everybody competes, nobody gets any points. If everybody cooperates, they get 90 each. However, if there is a mix of both, then competors get more than the cooperators. If the instructor desires, after a few rounds, the incentive to compete can be increased by changing 90 to 115 and 10 to 20 in the payoff formula.

After explaining the payoff matrix, have students fill out the blank decision forms (Figure 16.1 in their texts) or provide them with copies of the form reproduced at the end of this session's instructor notes. Allow a few minutes for completion and then collect them. Sort them into two piles, and calculate the score for competors and cooperators as per formula above. Draw three columns on the black board and complete the information pertaining to: round number, score for competors, and score for cooperators after each round.

After entering the scores on the board, randomly pick out a few decision slips from each pile and read out the reasons given without revealing the name of the student. Then allow a few minutes for the students to move around. Suggest to them that without revealing their decision in the previous round, they could discuss with each other the need to compete or cooperate. Usually, the cooperators, who score lower, take this opportunity to convince others of the need to cooperate so everyone's score goes up. . Distribute decision slips for each round.

At the end of the stipulated number of rounds, add the scores of the students and announce the name of the student or students who got the most points. If there are a large number of students in class, it would help to have a teaching assistant to calculate the individual scores of students while the exercise is being played. Alternatively, following an honor system, the students may be asked to announce their scores at the end of a session to identify the winners. These scores can always be checked from the decision slips with the instructor.

Debriefing

Open the class for discussion after Phase II. The main points around which the discussion can focus are:

1. The reasons for the students' decision to compete or cooperate?
2. What factors made them change the decision from one round to the next?
3. What information or situation would have helped them decide more easily to cooperate?
4. If the names of the competors or cooperators are announced during each round, how would that have affected the decision? (In the real world, the names of cooperators and competors are known.)

ASSESSMENT

To assess this session, have students answer the questions reproduced in the assessment form at the end of this session's instructor notes. Possible answers to these questions are given below.

1. What is the difference between a competitor and a complementor?

Answer: A player is a complementor if customers value a company's product more when they have the complementor's product than when they have the company's product alone. A player is a competitor if customers value a company's product less when they have the competitor's product.

2. Under what circumstances would a firm cooperate and compete with another at the same time?

Answer: (a) When the same product is a complementor and a competitor. A software developer writing a product that works on a Microsoft operating system enhances the value of the operating system by developing products for it and, therefore, is a complementor. At the same time, this software developer's product may compete with one of Microsoft's own products (for example, RealNetworks' RealJukebox vs. Microsoft Windows' Media Player). (b) When basic expertise is shared—for example, when manufacturers of CD players licensed the technology from Phillips and produced rival products. (c) When standards are established—for example, when Kodak and Fuji collaborated to develop smart film and compete against each other to sell it.

3. Can contracts between cooperators ensure that a common resource is not misused?

Answer: Contracts go a long way to ensure that responsibilities are delineated. Yet it is often very difficult to establish comprehensive systems of monitoring or to have a system of punishment for a violator. Moreover, the pressures of individual strategy to maximize returns for the individual players would mean taking advantage of a loophole in the contract to pursue individual benefit at the cost of a common resource. This problem of the individual vs. societal benefit transcends several fields. In the field of medicine, it is generally acknowledged that excessive use of antibiotics results in increased resistance to their efficacy. Nevertheless, individual medical practitioners find it difficult to resist prescribing it to alleviate the pain of their patients.

REFERENCES

Axelrod, R., W. Mitchell, R. E. Thomas, D. E. Bennett, and E. Bruderer. 1997. "Coalition forming in standard-setting alliances,'" In *The complexity of cooperation*, R. Axelrod, ed., 96–120. Princeton: Princeton University Press.

Brandenburgher, Adam M. and Barry J. Nalebuff. 1996. *Co-opetition*. New York: Currency Doubleday. *Note:* The attribution to Ray Noorda is provided in their book.

Klein, S. 1988. Classifying cooperative behavior. Paper presented at the Academy of International Business, San Diego, California, October 1988.

Decision Slip for Strategy Session 16

Name:	Round Number:

Decision: (Check one)

_____ I will compete and take 10 points higher than the cooperators.

_____ I will cooperate and accept 10 points lower that the competors.

Comment: Please briefly explain the reason for your decision.

Name:_____

ASSESSMENT FORM: STRATEGY SESSION 16

Instructions: Answer the following questions.

1. What is the difference between a competitor and a complementor?

_____

_____

_____

_____

_____

_____

_____

2. Under what circumstances would a firm cooperate and compete with another at the same time?

_____

_____

_____

_____

_____

_____

_____

_____

3. Can contracts between cooperators ensure that a common resource is not misused?

_____

_____

_____

_____

_____

_____

_____

_____

_____

Exercise: Whose Responsibility Is It?

OBJECTIVE

The social responsibility of business is explored as students examine the issue from two different perspectives. This session's exercise illustrates the impact of social responsibility on strategy implementation and can reinforce the stakeholder role in strategy formulation as well (see Strategy Session 5).

Time: 30–90 minutes

ADMINISTRATION

The time allocated for this exercise varies. The range is about 30 minutes for individual work to 90 minutes for team assignment.

Individual Basis

The exercise can be done in class on an individual basis. Allow 20 minutes for students to read the Global Chemical Company situation and answer the questions. Follow this with ten minutes of class discussion.

Team Assignment

Instruct students to read the Global Chemical case and answer the questions in the exercise before coming to class. Place the class into groups consisting of five or more students. In larger classes, where groups would consist of more than seven students, the instructor can either double up on stakeholder teams (for example, two separate groups taking the role of stockholders, and so on) or identify additional stakeholder groups (such as area businesses, lenders, or competitors). Assign individuals in each group to specific roles as follows:

1. Global Chemical management that holds the *activist viewpoint* towards social responsibility.
2. Global Chemical management with the *classical economic* viewpoint.
3. Stakeholder representation from the residents in the towns along the river in Kentucky.
4. The union at the plant.
5. Stockholders.

Assign each group a number as a form of identification. The task of member groups is to prepare a one-page memorandum to the Board of Directors. The memorandum should include:

1. A recommended course of action for the Board of Directors with the advantages and disadvantages of the recommended course of action.
2. A discussion of implementation issues.
3. A short comment about which stakeholders are being satisfied by this course of action.
4. What steps might be taken to deal with the other company stakeholders' concerns.

Allocate approximately 20 to 25 minutes for the development of the memorandums. Bring overhead slides on which teams write the memorandums or have them prepare the memorandums on computers in the classroom, if available. This facilitates the memorandum review process by the class. About five minutes before the groups have finished preparing their memorandums, ask each group to nominate one person from the group to move to a Board of Directors group that will select the "best" memorandum. All of the nominees will constitute the Board of Directors.

Each member of the newly formed Board of Directors group is given a copy of the rating sheet shown in Figure 17.1 to evaluate the groups' recommendations during the presentations. The criteria for evaluation are based on the four items listed above, plus additional criteria the Board may develop. The additional items are shared with the groups before the memorandums are completed. Examples of additional criteria are every member of the group must participation in the presentation of the memorandums and each group's recommendation should coincide with its stakeholder position.

As each group presents its recommendations, the Board members individually and separately score them on the rating sheet. Once the teams have presented their memorandums, the Board moves to the hallway or to another room to compare their ratings. Five minutes or so before the end of class, this group names the team that developed the best memorandum and the reason why they were chosen. Because each of the groups in class has a representative on the Board, they do not complain about the Board's decision.

Some reward for the group that the Board selects is strongly suggested. This might be bonus points for all members on a case or another assignment. For faculty who do not allocate bonus points, token rewards such as candy bars can be given to the team with the best memorandum, as chosen by the Board. As is often the case, one group stands out as having the best memorandum and is favored in the ratings by all members of the Board of Directors. However, if there is a close second, points or other rewards can be allocated accordingly. The fact that one group stands out, despite the self-interests of the Board members, illustrates the advantage of having detailed criteria against which to evaluate the memorandums. This can be applied to other areas, such as employee evaluation in the workplace and peer evaluations in the classroom.

ANSWERS TO EXERCISE QUESTIONS

The following are suggested answers to the questions that students must answer in the exercise.

1. Identify Global Chemical's stakeholders in this situation.

   Stakeholders are those individuals, groups, or organizations that have an interest or "stake" in the performance and success of an organization. At Global Chemical, these consist of the following:

   ▪ **Residents in towns along the river in Kentucky claiming pollutants from the Global Chemical plant are causing health problems.**

- Employees—half of the residents in Ashton, West Virginia, work at Global Chemical.
- Union at the plant (whose members are also employees).
- Area businesses such as the food stores and theaters whose sales depend on the spending patterns of Global Chemical employees.
- Suppliers who sell their products to Global Chemical, such as office suppliers and providers of raw materials.
- Creditors who have loaned money to Global Chemical.
- Local, state and federal governments that rely on residents in the community to pay taxes.
- Management and Global Chemical's Board of Directors who are responsible for the company's economic and social performance.
- Citizen environmental group that is concerned about the health hazards Global Chemical is causing.
- Stockholders—the owners of the company.

2. Whose responsibility is it to deal with the health concerns?

a. Classical economic approach

Those adopting the classical view of social responsibility would argue to leave the situation as is. Global Chemical exists to make profits, and as long as the company is not breaking any laws as it attempts to achieve its profit objectives, it is fulfilling its primary responsibility to the owners (stockholders). According to the classical view, government's responsibility is to change the laws that set pollution levels.

b. Activist approach

Those adopting the activist approach would favor taking a proactive approach to the problem. They would suggest that Global Chemical has the responsibility as a member of the community to be a concerned corporate citizen. On their own, they should be investigating ways to limit the level of pollutants, particularly since the filtering system is old. Given the company's resources (for example, engineers, scientists, legal counsel, and so on), the activist approach would favor having the company work with local and state governments to help solve the puzzle and limit the potential harm to community residents.

3. What are the company's alternatives?

a. Recommend no action be taken. The citizen environmental group has been complaining about the health hazards for two years without any proof that Global Chemical is causing the health problems. While the negative publicity could hurt Global Chemical's image in the community if a TV special were aired, Global Chemical can stand on its position that they are completely following the law regarding levels of pollution.

b. Recommend that the plant be closed and a new facility be identified overseas where environmental laws are less strict—and labor costs tend to be much lower. The cost of relocating will be offset by the lower operating costs. This alternative satisfies the citizen environmental group, the stockholders (since the company's stock price will probably not decline) and the company's management and Board of Directors, who are responsible for maintaining the company's level of profits. Employees, the Union, area businesses and local governments, however, would not be satisfied with this alternative.

c. Recommend a local site for a new facility using the same workforce. This alternative satisfies the greatest number of stakeholders: those who feel Global Chemical is responsible for the health hazards; employees who will not lose their jobs; area businesses who rely on Global employees for their patronage; suppliers and creditors who service Global Chemical's needs; and local governments that collect taxes from Global Chemical employees. Since the costs of relocation would not be offset by the lower costs noted in Alternative b., the stock market probably would not react favorably to the lower profits. Stockholders might sell their stock, thus lowering the price of the company's stock; management would be held accountable

4. Which alternative would you recommend? Which stakeholders are being satisfied by this decision?

Many students select Alternative c., relocate the plant in the local area. Ideally, this alternative demonstrates a company's concern for the greatest number of stockholders. However, the pressure to maintain profits is very strong and rarely do we see companies taking this type of action when it is at the expense of the stock price.

5. What specific steps would you suggest to deal with the other company stakeholder claims?

In terms of the stockholder claims and the need to maintain profits, management at Global Chemical might work with local and state government officials to gain tax incentives as a way to offset the high costs of relocating the plant in the local area (versus overseas). Other cost-cutting efforts such as shorter workweeks or lower pay raises might also keep profits from dropping below acceptable levels. Clearly, management's responsibility is to balance the need for profits and the company's social responsibility to its numerous stakeholders

ASSESSMENT: GROUP WORK EVALUATION

The **Group Work Evaluation** assessment form—reproduced at the end of this session's instructor notes—can be used to assess how well groups worked together on the assignment, particularly if you'd like feedback about how well the groups worked together. This form can be given to groups at the end of the session or at the start of the next class. If you want to analyze responses by groups, then make sure the students indicate the group number to which they belonged, without giving away their individual identities.

Make it clear that you want honest answers, and find a way to ensure that neither you nor other students can identify individual respondents. Summarize the ratings. Ask the groups themselves to suggest solutions to the concerns raised through the assessment.

Figure 17.1   Board of Director Group Rating Sheet

Rating System: 1 = Poor to 5 = Excellent

Group	Discussion of pros and cons for the course of action	How well were implementation issues addressed?	Connection between course of action and satisfied stakeholders	Steps suggested to deal with other company stakeholders	Other criteria identified by the Board	Other criteria identified by the Board
1						
2						
3						
4						
5						

Fill out the Group Work Evaluation circling a response or supplying an answer that most closely matches the opinion of your group.

Circle your group number: 1   2   3   4   5

1. Overall, how efficiently did your group work together on this assignment?

    Poorly   Adequately   Well   Extremely Well

2. Out of the five group members, how many participated actively most of the time?

    None   One   Two   Three   Four   All five

3. Out of the five group members, how many were prepared for the activity?

    None   One   Two   Three   Four   All five

4. Give one specific example of **something you learned from the group** that you probably would not have learned working alone.

    _____

    _____

    _____

    _____

5. Give one specific example of **something the other group members learned from you** that they probably would not have learned otherwise.

    _____

    _____

    _____

    _____

Lodging

Industry Profile

The lodging industry profile is included in the student text to illustrate the information a detailed industry survey should contain and how that information is organized. Although more information is available than ever from Internet, database, library, and other resources, many students are overwhelmed by the task of consolidating and organizing data. Therefore, this profile gives them an example of how to set up an industry study.

The information is briefly categorized this way:

- **Overview** A general definition of the industry, historical information about it, summary data about its size, and competitors within the industry.
- **Growth projections** A comparison of the size of the industry and forecasts for future growth.
- **Industry segments** Any grouping of segments or competitors that helps to define the industry structure.
- **Industry (seller) concentration** Tally of the number and size (sales) of competitors in the industry.
- **Trends** Discussion of changes in industry segments, marketing, new technology, and innovation
- **Industry outlook** Life-cycle information and any other projections concerning industry structure and conduct

This profile also provides an opportunity for students to apply the industry information to the Five Forces Model outlined in Strategy Session 6. Experience suggests that the more times students analyze industries using the Five Forces Model, the better they understand competition and the nature of strategy development. As shown in Table A.1, the lodging industry is becoming more concentrated and threats from other forces are low, causing competitors to earn high profits.

OPTIONAL STRATEGIC GROUP ANALYSIS

An optional assignment for students is to research characteristics of firms in the lodging industry and to place them into various strategic groupings. Strategic groups consist of those rival firms with similar competitive approaches and positions in the market, and analyzing competition using this framework is another way to understand the industry.

Most industries contain subsets of firms that are strategically similar in terms of the market segments they serve, price, quality, technological leadership, distribution channels, or any factors that influence success. For example, although Howard Johnson and the very upscale Claridge Hotel in Chicago are part of the same lodging industry, they have different missions, objectives, and strategies and belong to different strategic groups. They have very little in common and pay little attention to each other when planning competitive actions. However, Holiday Inn and Howard Johnson have a great deal in common in terms of their similar strategy of building economy-type properties and targeting families. Consequently, they are strong rivals, and the competitive actions of one closely affect sales and profits of the other.

Table A.1   Five Forces Model

Force	Lodging Industry
Rivalry among existing firms	*Medium/Low.* Rivalry is becoming less intense as lodging companies continue to consolidate and account for larger percentages of industry sales than in previous years (Marriott—$8 billion; Cendant Corp—$5.1 billion; Starwood Hotels—$4.7 billion; Accor—$3.2 billion; Bass Hotels—$1.4 billion; Promus—$1.1 billion).
Barriers to entry	*Medium/High.* Entry into the industry as a standalone property is more difficult due to the trend of hotels becoming members of chains. Standalone properties lack the brand recognition and economies of scale enjoyed by the chains, thus making entry difficult.
Bargaining power of suppliers	*Low.* The number of employees per 100 occupied rooms has dropped 10% during the past 10 years due to laborsaving devices such as automated check-in and checkout services. Other suppliers, such as furniture and equipment sellers, are numerous, and switching costs are low.
Bargaining power of buyers	*Low/Medium.* The "low" rating is associated more with end consumers (individuals) who are not able to negotiate major deals with lodging companies. The buyers are fragmented and therefore do not have negotiating power. Business customers, travel agents, conference organizers, AAA, however, have more influence. They have greater leverage, given the choices in hotels and the fact that switching costs are low.
Substitutes	*Low.* Travelers on vacation could stay with friends or family as a substitute for staying at a hotel or motel. Business firms might provide either their own accommodation as part of the business enterprise or own an apartment for this purpose. However, these options are not a major threat. At one time, teleconferencing was predicted as a substitute for traveling to other locations for business purposes (thus, eliminating overnight stays). This has not materialized as a major threat to the industry.
Relative power of other stakeholders	*Low.* In this industry, other stakeholders such as the Federal or state governments are not a major factor affecting the profit potential of the industry.

The groups can be "mapped" by plotting the market positions of industry competitors on a graph using two strategic variables. A number of variables can be chosen; and it is not unusual for management to create several maps with different strategic variables for an industry analysis. The Figure A.1 below shows the type of property as one dimension and market segmentation as the other. These variables were chosen, since competitors in this industry increasingly are turning to market segmentation as competitive strategy.

Another map might compare the ownership structure of firms—that is, individual versus chain—and location. Given the increased consolidation of the industry and chain affiliation, this represents another important competitive consideration. When creating these maps, the two variables selected as axes should not be closely related. If they are, the circles on the map fall along the diagonal, and strategy makers learn nothing more than if they considered only one variable. In addition, the variables used as axes do not have to be either quantitative or continuous. They can be discrete variables (as used in Figure A.1). Circle sizes drawn proportional to the sales of the firms in each group allows the map to reflect the relative size of the strategic groups.

In summary, strategic groups provide management with information about how companies within the same industry might differ from each other and what implications these differences have for future strategy. If threats are stronger in one group than another from the risk of potential entrants, bargaining power of buyers or suppliers, etc., then managers must evaluate several possibilities. Would the firm be better off competing in a different strategic group or are the costs associated with movement, because of mobility barriers between groups, too high? In terms of growth and the addition of new properties, is one group more favorable than another?

Figure A.1   Type of Property and Market Segmentation*

High-end

Group A
Claridge, Chicago;
XV Beacon, Boston;
Bryant Park, NY

Group C
Promus (Doubletree
Hotels, Embassy Suites);
Carlson Group (Raddison)

**Type of
Property**

Group D
Cendant (Days Inn,
Super 8, Howard
Johnson, Travelodge);
Bass (Holiday Inn)

Group B
LaQuinta Motor Inn

Economy

Business Travelers   **Market Segmentation**   Families

---

* *Time.* 2000. Creature comforts. *Time* (May 8) 155(19): B16–19.

This information systems (IS) industry profile is provided as a contrast to the lodging industry. The IS industry is a dynamic and rapidly changing one and presents a challenge for students to analyze. The information provided in the IS profile in the student text is meant to be indicative and is not a comprehensive coverage of the industry. This industry fascinates students because most of them have grown up seeing the many IS products and services that have emerged in the past two decades. There are three ways in which the IS profile can be used: with the Five Forces Model or the Game Theory approach—or in a project.

FIVE FORCES MODEL

Students find a particular challenge in identifying the industry when applying Porter's model. The industry is expanding rapidly with distinct segments emerging and the term "IS industry" means many things to many people. The instructor can explore the definition and boundaries of the industry as a useful way of illustrating its complexity. Yet, it is an important first step to define the boundaries of the industry to conduct a meaningful analysis. Note, however, that trying to apply the model to the entire IS industry is not recommended given that the nature of competition and the impact of the forces are unique within each segment. For example, the composition of rivalry and substitutes, and the distinction between entry and mobility barriers would all change depending on the industry definition. Table B.1 applies the Five Forces Model to the personal computer (PC) industry. It illustrates how examining the "Hardware" industry, which includes PCs, could dilute the power of the analysis.

The conclusion from the above shows that the PC industry is not attractive—although the picture is not clear for the hardware industry.

Students often choose to analyze the PC industry since they are most familiar with it.

Although the note does not provide much information on "suppliers," students are aware of the power of microprocessor manufacturers (for example, Intel and AMD) and this can be factored into the discussion. In the case of "buyers," the PC industry uses direct sales and retail stores, both general and specialty, for distribution. The stores have power since several PC makers are viewed as comparable in quality and price, the role of the store is important for sales, and can therefore bargain for higher margins. When the buyer is the end consumer, as in the case of Dell and Gateway who sell directly, there is less power per individual consumer to affect pricing.

Recent cases such as the antitrust suit against Microsoft and the court decision upholding certain software patents show the emergent nature of the industry and the influence of regulatory authorities in determining it. In addition, the debates on Internet privacy and security of data and the question of taxes related to e-commerce show that significant changes are yet to come. All these argue in favor of including "stakeholders" as a sixth force in the model.

If the profile is used for the purpose of exploring the Five Forces Model, it would be advisable to get the students to read the note prior to coming to class. In class, students working in groups can undertake the analysis, followed by general debriefing.

Table B.1   Five Forces Model Applied to the PC Industry

Force	PC Industry	Hardware
Barriers to entry	*Low.* Ease of purchasing components and assembling makes entry relatively free. However, short product cycle may serve to deter entrants.	*Medium/High.* Proprietary technologies, and R&D requirements serve as barriers in the case of mainframes and servers.
Bargaining power of suppliers	*High.* Intel dominates the market. Alternatives available from AMD, etc., yet their acceptance is not as wide as that of Intel.	*Medium.* Large players in industry, some of whom have captive microprocessor manufacturing capabilities.
Bargaining power of buyers	*Medium/High.* Large buyers are able to negotiate deals. Individuals have a variety to choose from.	Some power with buyers of high-end specialized machines (supercomputers).
Rivalry	*High.* Increasing concentration, and slowing growth results in intense fight for market share.	Varying impacts in each segment.
Substitutes	*Low/Medium.* Macintosh machines, "Internet appliances" to access WWW, email, etc. are substitutes for narrow applications.	*High.* PCs are networked and some workstations substitute for mainframes.
Stakeholders/Regulatory authorities	*Low.* No apparent concerns.	Low. No apparent concerns.

GAME THEORY APPROACH

Unlike Porter's model that is based on micro-economic theory, an alternative model called the "Value Net" uses game theory to build in competition and cooperation in examining a firm's strategic choices within an industry (see Instructor's Notes for Strategy Session 16: The Role of Cooperation in Strategic Management). A company may choose to cooperate with some players and compete with others, or with the same firm on different aspects. Thus, Kodak and Fuji compete fiercely in the film market and cooperate in the development of advanced film technology. From this perspective, the company is in the center of a value net and has to deal with customers, suppliers, competitors and complementors.

In the IS industry, we see several examples of competition and cooperation. For example, Intel and Microsoft cooperate since one company's products are valued more when the customer has the other's products. Thus, they are complementors. As technology changes and new product uses emerge, the range of opportunities available in the industry alters and with it the position of competitors and complementors can change. IBM and Microsoft were cooperating at one time on the OS/2 operating system, which changed to competition between Windows and OS/2 when Microsoft changed its strategy.

PROJECT

A third use of the IS industry profile is to assign it as a starting point for a more thorough industry analysis (see Part V: Semester Projects, in the student text). Students can be asked to research the library or the Internet for additional data about a segment within it. The Five Forces Model can then be applied on the segment being focused. In addition, the product life cycle can be used to examine why some markets grow rapidly and then taper off, such as the ERP segment (see the PeopleSoft case in Strategy Session 15) or the slowing growth in the PC segment.

ASSESSMENT

If the instructor uses the profile to illustrate application of the Five Forces Model or the Game Theory, two approaches are recommended. In one, the instructor can collect the application of the model (whether done in class or as homework) and grade it on the extent to which the student has correctly associated information from the profile to illustrate each element of the model. In the second approach, the instructor can ask the student to write and turn in answers to the following questions at the beginning of the next class. (A printed form is supplied at the end of these instructor notes.)

1. Identify one element from the model discussed. What was the conclusion about the impact of the force/element on the industry?
2. Identify another industry where this element has the opposite influence on the firm.
3. How should a firm in industry 1 and 2 above incorporate the above information in its strategy?

Answer: If the industry considered for 1 is the PC industry, the table above suggests that the threat of entry is high. As a contrast, the industry for 2 could be microprocessors, where the threat of entry is low, due to patent issues, high costs of R&D, high capital expenditure (a minimum efficient size of plant is estimated at about $1 billion), and existing excess capacity. Thus, the strategy of a player in the PC industry would have to include efforts to create brand loyalty to withstand the pressures by constant new entrants into the industry. The players in the microprocessor industry would instead use resources to enhance product development, and the like, and they are not worried about entry issues keeping a pressure on prices.

When the profile is used as a starting point for a more elaborate student project, then the instructor may use a separate set of guidelines for the project rather than test the specific use made of this profile.

REFERENCES

Brandenburger, Adam and Barry Nalebuff. 1996. Co-opetition, New York: Doubleday.

Wheelen, Thomas L., and J. David Hunger. 1998. *Strategic Management*. Reading, MA: Addison-Wesley.

Name:_____

ASSESSMENT FORM: INFORMATION SYSTEMS INDUSTRY PROFILE

Directions: Please respond to the questions below.

1. Identify one element from the model discussed. What was the conclusion about the impact of the force/element on the industry?

_____

_____

_____

_____

_____

_____

_____

_____

2. Identify another industry where this element has the opposite influence on the firm.

_____

_____

_____

_____

_____

_____

_____

_____

3. How should a firm in industry 1 and 2 above incorporate the above information in its strategy?

_____

_____

_____

_____

_____

_____

_____

_____

MICA

Method of Case Analysis and Discussion

To help students understand case discussion using the MICA method, schedule a demonstration of the method in which the instructor plays the roll of the administrative team.

DEMONSTRATION

1. Briefly describe a hypothetical case. An example is given below.

   Eastern University has four colleges: Engineering; Business, Arts and Sciences; and Law. The institution borrowed extensively to meet expenses over the last two years. The engineering college has experienced declining enrollment for six years, and applications for the upcoming year are at the lowest point in that college's history. The other colleges have steady enrollment.

   Academic consultants prepared a series of recommendations, one of which was to start a nursing school in January 2005. The cost was estimated at $85,000 for a faculty position, $7,000 for special laboratory equipment, $5,000 for marketing expenses. Several professors suggested that the engineering college should switch to a totally distance learning format, with the industrial engineering major the first to changeover. Costs were estimated at $2,000,000 for start-up (extensive technology revamping and faculty development grants) and $300,000 for yearly maintenance expenses. The dean of the engineering college argued instead for a new offsite campus facility in the western part of the state where two or three classes would be held in a large employer's facility. The marketing department suggested a new advertising campaign targeted at engineering students (costing $140,000), which would bring in additional students. Employees in admissions suggested that two more assistants be hired ($85,000) and that an open-admissions policy be created where new students are accepted all year for all of the colleges at the university (rather than just in April and May).

2. Hand out to students the sample sheet of action steps reproduced at the end of these instructor notes for the MICA method.

   Advise the class that preparation of this type of sheet is the responsibility of the administrative team. They are to collect action steps from each student and compile these steps for the case discussion. Depending on the class size, limit the number of action steps that can be submitted by any one student to one strategic-level and one operational-level course of action. The administrative team compiles similar recommendations into one summary step and lists author names after the step.

   Regarding the grouping of action steps into strategic versus operational categories, in the early stages of the case method, students in the class and the administrative teams have difficulty distinguishing between the two. Therefore, for the first few cases, help the administrative team with the grouping. Also, as is frequently the case, if a student submits two operational-level steps (even though one is labeled *strategic*), the administrative team accepts only one operational-level course of action.

Point out how important it is to discuss strategic steps first. For example, if the class votes to accept Strategic Step 1, then Operational Step 4a is no longer valid. It would have been a waste of time to discuss action step 4a before Strategic Step 1 (an opportune time to point out that strategic-level decisions drive those at the operational level, which is also the point in Strategy Session 1).

For the demonstration case, many of the suggested courses of action are given in the case. However, we advise students that most cases do not provide detailed recommendations, and they are responsible for developing these. Note steps 1, 4b, and 8 are original ideas.

3. Run through the case.

    Acting as the chairperson, the instructor follows the process described in Part V of the student text. The instructor also takes on the students' role to demonstrate the kind of discussion that earns points. The instructor can give an example—such as the student who says, "I agree with what Mr. Smith said."—and then explain why this earns the student no points, based on item C in Figure C.1.

4. Charts for scoring.

    A seating chart for scoring purposes has been created. One is for grading (Figure C.2), and the other (Figure C.3) is given to the administrative team so that the counter can keep track of how many times each student is called on to participate. These are simply reversed charts. Spaces are left in each box to allow for slash marks to indicate number of points earned (instructor's grading chart) and the number of times students were called on (counter's record).

Figure C.1   Selected MICA Grading Criteria

A. The comment must be relevant to the specific action step being discussed.
B. The comment must contain a supportive argument (because . . .).
C. The comment must not be a repeat of what was said before.
D. Single comments have the following point values:

1 point	Ordinary, but relevant comment.
2 points	Insightful comment that points out consequences of taking or not taking the action.
3–4 points	When financial ratio analysis is included in the comment (or any theory or concept from class discussion).

E. Bonus points may be awarded based on outside published research or interviews with persons knowledgeable about the subject matter.
F. Members of the administrative team each earn the number of points earned by the highest scorer in the class, provided the team has performed the duties and has not been penalized by a discrimination charge.

Figure C.2   Front of Room Chart for Instructor's Grading

Sentro		Roy		Stone	Harve
Rodriquez	Williamson		Nogueira	Johnson	Rummell
Stanlick	McLod		Jeffreys	Silvestori	James
Patrino		Deyo	Clarke		Smith
				Instructor	

Figure C.3   Back of Room Chart for Administrative Team

	Instructor				
Smith		Clarke	Deyo		Patrino
James	Silvestori	Jeffreys		McLod	Stanlick
Rummell	Johnson	Nogueira		Williamson	Rodriquez
Harve	Stone		Roy		Sentro

GRADED CASE DISCUSSIONS

Once the graded case discussions begin, particularly in the first two cases, intervene on procedural and content issues to set the tone. However, this is not necessary as the semester progresses, since the administrative teams quickly take on this role.

Throughout the semester, during the last five or ten minutes of the session, review issues that were either dealt with inappropriately in the discussion or were not dealt with at all but were crucial in the case.

Action Steps: Eastern University Case

STRATEGIC ACTION STEPS

1. Close the engineering college by Fall 2004. (Smith, Clarke, Rodriguez, Patrino)
2. Convert engineering college to a distance-learning format, starting with the industrial engineering major Fall 2003. Cost is $2,000,000 for start-up and $300,000 for yearly expenses. (James, Deyo, Nogueira)
3. Start a nursing school in January 2005. Costs are $85,000 for a faculty position, $7,000 for special laboratory equipment, $5,000 for marketing. (Rumell)

OPERATIONAL ACTION STEPS

4. Implement a marketing campaign:
   a. For the engineering college. Cost is $140,000. (Deyo, Patrino, Nogueira)
   b. For the entire university—cost estimated at $450,000. (Roy)
5. Accept applications for admissions into all of the colleges any time during the year. (Silvestori, McLod)
6. Open an off-campus site for engineering courses at the employer's facility by September 2002 (estimated cost $30,000 for a director and $8,000 for supplies). (James, Johnson)
7. Hire two more admissions assistants at a cost of $85,000 by the end of this academic year. (Stanlick, Clarke)
8. Lower tuition by $1,000 to $17,000 per year. (Williamson)

NOTE FOR FUTURE CASES

Submit two action steps that briefly summarize your recommendation about WHAT the company should do—one action step at the strategic level and the other at the operational level. Do not submit information discussing WHY the company should follow your recommendation. Save that for in-class discussion.

Be specific about WHAT you are recommending so that the class can vote on it. Provide costs and dates, as much as possible. For example, an action step to "improve marketing" is not specific, and it would be difficult for the class to discuss and vote on this course of action.

Appendix A

Team Formation

Several courses require student activity in teams that lasts throughout the semester. Quite often, however, the teams formed by the instructor or students are provided with little assistance on how to work as a team. The format described below is meant to help students develop their own norms and objectives to accomplish team activity and has been found to work very well.

PHASE I

Formation

Some instructors prefer to form the teams themselves. Others allow students to form the teams but specify criteria and retain a veto power if a team does not satisfy the norms. It is useful, for example, to require diversity in the team. Diversity can be defined to mean:

1. Students of different majors should be represented.
2. No two students from the same organization or (non-U.S.) country of origin should be on the team.

In addition, allow the students about 15 minutes to walk around and form the teams based on the criteria specified.

A third option is to permit students to team up with one other person, and then the instructor forms the rest of the group. Lastly, for those students who do not know others in the class, offer the option of a random pooling of names. With these options, request that student pairings or random pool preference be submitted by the next class.

Team Size

This can depend on the number of students in the class and the activities that the team engages in. Team sizes of three or four work best.

PHASE II

Once the teams are formed, they sit together and exchange telephone numbers and email addresses. Then they are asked to discuss and identify a common day and time of the week when they can meet. (In cases where the class is composed of a majority of part-time students, this can also be stipulated at the team selection stage discussed in Phase I). This is especially important if the team is going to undertake a project that will require regular meetings outside class.

Allow a ten-minute discussion within the teams of various good and bad team behaviors they have experienced in the past.

Conduct a general class debriefing for about ten minutes, asking each team to share one or two experiences with the whole class. The instructor, at this stage, can set up two columns on the board listing the good and bad team behaviors.

PHASE III

At the conclusion of the discussion in described in Phase II, ask the teams to make their own list of what they would agree as being recommended and prohibited behaviors within the team. Instruct them to prepare a contract, signed by all members of the team, and a copy of this signed contract to be submitted to the instructor. The contract should contain the following:

1. The team's objective. This could be a learning objective or a grade in the course.
2. Their selected meeting day and time.
3. How they propose to conduct and regulate themselves.

Appendix B

When activities are undertaken as a team, it is advisable to inform the students at the beginning of the semester that a peer evaluation form will be administered at the end of the semester and their response will be used to translate group grades to individual grades. A model for this form is reproduced on the next facing page.

149

CONFIDENTIAL PEER EVALUATION FORM

Section:_____

Your Name: _____ Group: _____

Use this form to evaluate the contribution made by each of your group members to the overall performance and success of your group's projects. In making your assessments, you might take into account such factors as:

a. Effort
b. Quantity of contribution
c. Quality of contribution
d. Evidence of advance preparation for meetings
e. Meeting of deadlines
f. Degree of cooperation with other group members
g. Other criteria developed as part of your team contract

DIRECTIONS

1. In the space provided below, write the names of all group members (including yourself).
2. Allocate a total of 100 points among your group members (including yourself) such that the points awarded indicate your judgment of the overall value of each member's relative contribution. **The total points awarded must add up to 100.**

   For example, if you have five group members and, in your judgment, all members made equal contributions, each group member (including yourself) would be allocated 20 points. If you awarded someone 10 points and someone else 30 points, this would indicate that you valued the latter person's contribution three times more than the first person's contribution.

3. Write a brief paragraph about each group member's contributions to your semester's work on the back of this sheet.
4. While making your assessment, keep in mind all group-based activities performed during the semester.

Group Member Names	Points
a.	
b.	
c.	
d.	
Total	**100 points**

Your instructor will keep the information on this form confidential.